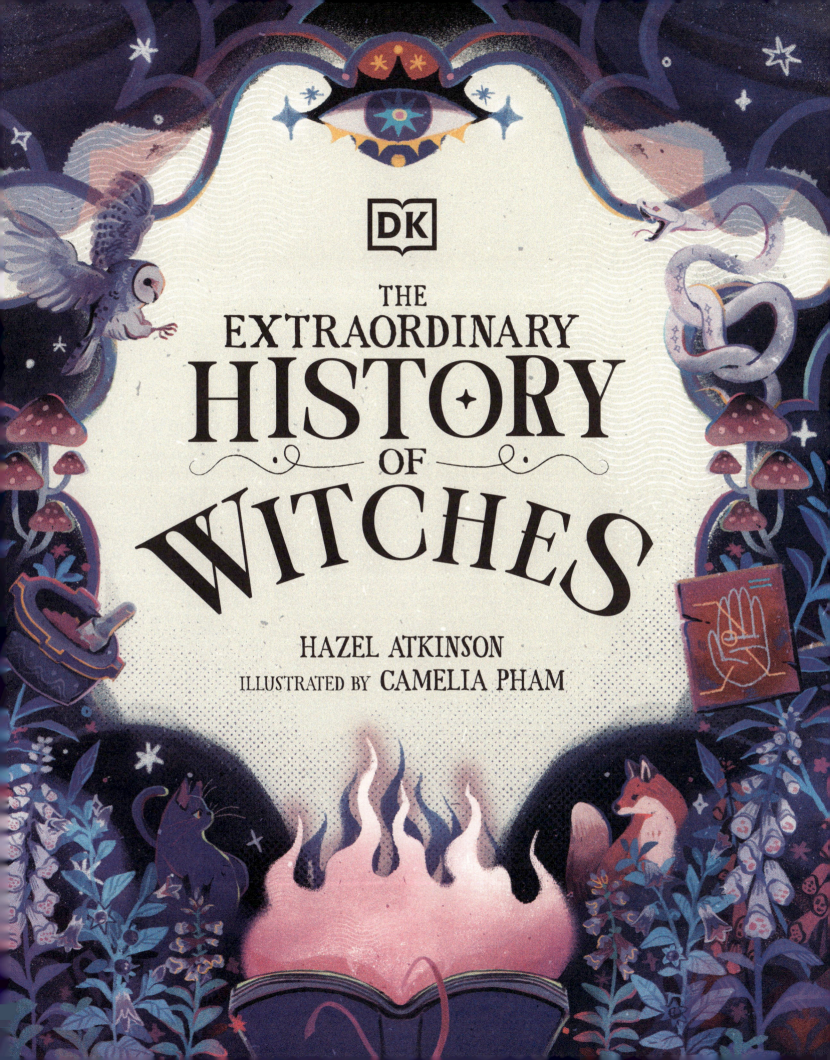

Written by Hazel Atkinson
Illustrated by Camelia Pham

Consultant Professor Diane Purkiss

Project Editor Sophie Parkes
Editorial Assistant Francesca Harper
Editor Sarah Bailey
Senior US Editor Megan Douglass
Senior Art Editor Charlotte Bull
Designers Sophie Gordon, Holly Price
Managing Editor Penny Smith
Managing Art Editor Elle Ward
Production Editor Anita Yadav
Picture Research Geetam Biswas
Production Controller Inderjit Bhullar
Jacket Designer Elle Ward
Associate Publishing Director Francesca Young
Art Director Mabel Chan

First American Edition, 2025
Published in the United States by DK Publishing,
a division of Penguin Random House LLC
1745 Broadway, 20th Floor, New York, NY 10019

Text copyright © Hazel Atkinson 2025
Artwork copyright © Camelia Pham 2025
Layout and design copyright © 2025
Dorling Kindersley Limited
25 26 27 28 29 10 9 8 7 6 5 4 3 2 1
001-345379-Aug/2025

All rights reserved.
Without limiting the rights under the copyright reserved above, no part of this publication may be reproduced, stored in or introduced into a retrieval system, or transmitted, in any form, or by any means (electronic, mechanical, photocopying, recording, or otherwise), without the prior written permission of the copyright owner. DK values and supports copyright. Copyright fuels creativity, encourages diverse voices, promotes free speech, and creates a vibrant culture. Thank you for buying an authorized edition of this publication and for complying with copyright laws by not reproducing, scanning, or distributing any part of it in any form without permission. You are supporting writers and artists and allowing DK to continue to publish books that inform and inspire readers.
No part of this publication may be used or reproduced in any manner for the purpose of training artificial intelligence technologies or systems. In accordance with Article 4(3) of the DSM Directive 2019/790, DK expressly reserves this work from the text and data mining exception.

Published in Great Britain by Dorling Kindersley Limited
ISBN: 978-0-5939-6551-1

DK books are available at special discounts when purchased in bulk for sales promotions, premiums, fund-raising, or educational use.
For details, contact: DK Publishing Special Markets,
1745 Broadway, 20th Floor, New York, NY 10019
SpecialSales@dk.com

Printed and bound in China

www.dk.com

CONTENTS

Chapter One
DEFINING WITCHES

What is a witch?....................8
Are all witches women?....................10
Witch stereotypes....................12
Timeline of witchcraft....................14
Magic, religion, and witchcraft....................16
Legends around the world....................18

Chapter Two
ANCIENT ORIGINS

Ancient sources....................22
Mesopotamian magic....................24
Egyptian magic....................26
Muslims and magic....................28
Chinese magic....................30
Empress Chen Jiao....................32
Japanese magic....................34
Greek magic....................36
Circe....................38
Roman magic....................40
Magical plants....................42
Curses....................44
Medea....................46
Love spells and potions....................48

This book was made with Forest Stewardship Council™ certified paper—one small step in DK's commitment to a sustainable future. Learn more at www.dk.com/uk/information/sustainability

Chapter Three
RELIGION, MYTHS, AND MAGIC

The medieval mind......................................52
European witches......................................54
Norse magic..56
Fairy tales and folklore.............................58
Creatures of the night..............................60
Protective charms.....................................62
Growing magic..64
Witch's toolkit...66
Divination...68
Modes of transportation...........................70
Celtic magic..72
Alice Kyteler..74
Magical healers and cunning folk.............76
Vodou...78

Chapter Four
A WORLD OF NEW IDEAS

The rise of witch hunts..............................82
European witch trials................................84
Joan of Arc...86
Methods of trying a witch.........................88
Witch hunters...90
The Sabbath..92
Mexican Inquisition...................................94
Colonialism and witchcraft........................96
Magical objects...98
Pendle witch trials...................................100

Salem witch trials....................................102
What caused the witch hunts?................104
North America and magic........................106
African witchcraft...................................108
Shape-shifters and familiars....................110

Chapter Five
A NEW AGE

An age of enlightenment?.......................114
Modern beliefs..116
Occultism and spiritualism......................118
Magical men..120
Brujeria...122
Wicca..124
Tarot...126
The magic of crystals..............................128
The witch in modern media....................130
Witches fight back..................................132
Green witchcraft.....................................134
The future of witches.............................136

What does "witch" mean to you?...........138

Glossary..140
Index...142
Acknowledgments...................................144

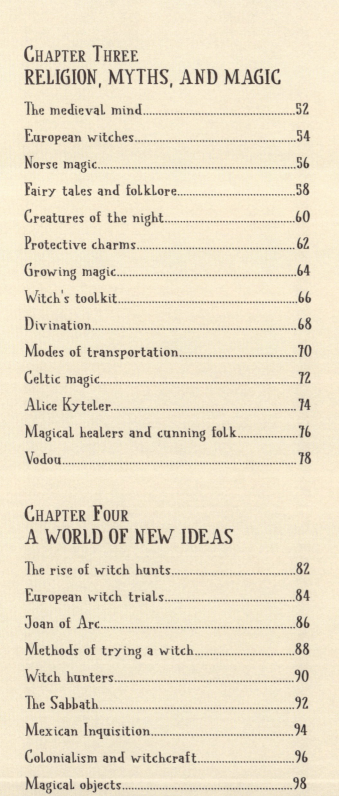

Foreword

Welcome to a world of dreams and visions; of stories and imaginings; of darkness and light. A world of witches ...

Throughout history, most societies have imagined witches—powerful users of magic who can change things around them for good or bad. Sometimes, as you will learn, those stories ended up being applied to real women—most of whom were just living difficult lives on the margins of society.

Whenever we imagine and whenever we tell stories, we like scaring ourselves! Witches have often been scary because they are powerful. As you learn about witches, you will understand that power is not good or bad by itself, but can be used for good or bad purposes. You too can make your own stories about witches; stories about power; stories about fear.

You too can be as curious as a black cat.

And you too can dream of flying!

Professor Diane Purkiss
Consultant

Introduction

For as long as we have believed in magic, we have told stories of those who could wield it. None of these figures are more mysterious than the witch. From the dark woods of Russia to the sunlit streets of Mexico, witches appear in the history and folklore of almost every culture around the world. But what is a "witch?" And why are we so enchanted by them?

In this book we will journey through time to uncover the extraordinary history of witches. The stories we will uncover are complicated. They can be dark and upsetting at times, but they also represent resistance, resilience, and the courage to stand out and be yourself.

I hope you enjoy learning about this magical subject. As for "what is a witch?" I'll leave that for you to decide!

Hazel Atkinson
Author

Chapter One

DEFINING WITCHES

Before we delve into the extraordinary history of witches, it's important to understand that "witch" doesn't have just one definition—just like the word "magic," it means something different to everyone! This book contains both made-up witches, from fairy tales and myths and legends, and real people, who have believed they are witches or who have been accused of witchcraft. This chapter will challenge some of the ideas you might already have about witches, and might answer some of the questions you've wanted to ask.

WHAT is a WITCH?

We have always been fascinated by witches. Around the world, stories full of magic and wonder have been shared, featuring powerful enchantresses and fearsome crones. Belief in witches also plays an important part in our history: many innocent people have suffered due to accusations that they have dabbled in harmful magic. But what exactly is a "witch?" Have you ever wondered ...

WHERE DO WITCHES COME FROM?

ARE WITCHES REAL OR IMAGINARY?

WHO BELIEVES IN WITCHES?

ARE WITCHES GOOD OR EVIL?

ARE WITCHES OLD OR YOUNG?

ARE WITCHES MALE OR FEMALE?

ARE ALL WITCHES WOMEN?

Stories of magic are as old as humanity, and evidence of belief in witches has even been discovered in some of the earliest known examples of writing. However, it can be hard to define exactly what a "witch" is. The majority of people accused of witchcraft have been women. Even today, a typical image of a witch shows her as an old woman with a pointy hat and a broomstick. But why?

The link between women and witchcraft can be traced all the way back to ancient Mesopotamia, when it was assumed in many texts that witches were female. In the literature of ancient Greece and Rome, harmful magic was often performed by women, and in ancient China, the power of the *wu* was associated with women under the Zhou dynasty. These older beliefs influenced writers in early modern Europe, who combined them with ideas about the nature of women, so that by the 15th century, women and witchcraft were firmly linked.

In the early modern period, you were far more likely to be accused of witchcraft if you were a woman. In England, 90 percent of those accused were women, and this trend was common around the world. This does not mean that only women could be accused of witchcraft—in some northern and eastern European countries, including Iceland, Finland, and Russia, most of those tried were male.

Bewitching women

Historic ideas about the nature of women and witches made it more likely that women would be accused. They were seen as weaker than men, as well as greedy, jealous, and sly. This was thought to make them more likely to give in to evil. Witchcraft was also seen as a secretive crime that happened behind closed doors, and might involve hurting animals, spoiling milk, making children sick, or causing food to rot. Since women were more involved in household work, it was more likely they would be suspected. Vulnerable women, such as the elderly, poor, or unmarried, were most at risk, because they were seen as burdens to society. While most of the accused were innocent, some women could use the label of "witch" to their advantage, holding fear and respect within their communities.

The accusers

We know that women were more likely to be suspected of witchcraft, but who was accusing them? Most accusations took place within villages, where tension between neighbors could build up over years before exploding. Accusers were most often women, supported by male witnesses. However, during the early modern period men usually held the positions of power, so it would be men who passed the judgment at trial.

WITCH STEREOTYPES

A stereotype is an idea of something that is overly simple or exaggerated. When we imagine a witch, we often rely on stereotypes to form an image in our heads. Films, TV, and books have influenced these ideas, but many stereotypes are deeply rooted in the history of witchcraft, and can be traced back hundreds of years.

"Witches look different!"
This idea comes from early modern Europe, and its harmful beliefs about people who looked different. Natural marks on the body, such as warts or birthmarks, were thought to "prove" their owner was a witch.

"Witches are old!"
You might picture a witch as wrinkly or crooked. This is because in early modern Europe, older women were more likely to be accused of witchcraft. However, the ancient Greeks imagined witches as young enchantresses, while others associated magic with middle-aged men whose gifts came from studying ancient texts.

"Witches are evil!"
In most cultures, witches have been seen as evil people who practice bad magic. They might call down storms, destroy crops, cause animals to become sick, or ask demons to do their bidding. However, some witches practice good magic that helps rather than harms.

"Witches ride on broomsticks!"
The idea of witches flying across the sky is found in many cultures. While some travel by broom, others use more unusual means, such as a mortar and pestle or a stalk of grass. Some cultures believed witches could transform themselves into monsters and soar on wings.

"Witches have green skin!"
This idea is much newer, because witches weren't shown with green skin until 1939! In the film *The Wizard of Oz*, costume designers decided that the sickly color made the Wicked Witch of the West look scary. It also showed up well on film!

"Witches love black cats!"
Black cats and witches go hand in hand. But why? In early modern Britain, people believed that witches had "familiars"—demons, usually in animal form, who would help a witch. Black cats were popular, but they might also keep dogs, mice, birds, or even insects.

"Witches live alone!"
In popular folk tales, witches can be found living alone in magical, mystical homes. Historically, women living alone, such as widows, were more vulnerable to accusations of witchcraft. In Indigenous American cultures, those who practiced dark magic were also people who lived apart from society.

TIMELINE of WITCHCRAFT

The history of witchcraft spans not only centuries, but millennia too, and can be traced to every country on the globe, one way or another. This timeline should give you a sense of just how vast and rich the history of witchcraft is, and will introduce you to some of the things that will be covered in this book.

10,000-2200 BCE
During the Neolithic period, prehistoric peoples use magic and rituals to make sense of the world around them.

c. 700 BCE
Laws against witchcraft are found in Jewish religious texts, including Exodus, Leviticus, and Deuteronomy.

c. 1000 BCE
The Mesopotamian *Maqlu* texts are written. These tablets contain spells and rituals for fighting witchcraft.

c. 700-600 BCE
Homer writes the *Odyssey*. In this ancient poem, the Greek hero Odysseus faces the enchantress Circe.

c. 449 BCE
The Twelve Tables, a set of laws, are published in Rome. They include rules against using magic for evil.

c. 130 BCE
Empress Chen Jiao is put on trial for witchcraft in China along with many accomplices. She is exiled from court.

c. 60 BCE
The Romans found Aquae Sulis, now known as Bath, a spa town in Britain. They leave curse tablets in the sacred springs, wishing harm on their enemies.

1482 CE
Christopher Columbus sails across the Atlantic Ocean and "discovers" America. The following colonization changes the world. Colonizers fail to understand Indigenous peoples' beliefs, accusing them of dark magic.

1324 CE
Alice Kyteler becomes the first person tried for witchcraft in Ireland, along with her companions.

1486 CE
The *Malleus Maleficarum* or "Hammer of the Witches" is published. This book teaches people how to hunt and identify "witches," and links women and witchcraft together.

1623-1631 CE
In Bamberg, Germany, as many as 900 people are accused and executed in witch trials.

1660 CE
The Royal Society for science is founded in England. Scientific discoveries are praised and encouraged. Skepticism about witchcraft increases.

1612 CE
At the Pendle witch trials in the English county of Lancashire, 12 people are accused of witchcraft.

1645-1647 CE
Under the judgment of so-called Witchfinder General Matthew Hopkins, hundreds of people are accused of witchcraft in the East Anglia witch trials during the unstable period of the English Civil War.

1692 CE
During the Salem witch trials, hysteria grips Salem Village, Massachusetts, and 19 people are executed for witchcraft.

1590 CE
At the North Berwick witch trials, a group of Scottish "witches" are accused of trying to kill King James VI of Scotland.

c. 1526-1827 CE
The Atlantic Slave Trade sees more than 12.5 million African men, women, and children enslaved and transported to the Americas to work on plantations. This leads to the creation of religions such as *Santeria* and *Vodou*. These are mistaken by European colonizers for witchcraft.

1735 CE
The Witchcraft Act of 1735 makes it a crime to claim to practice witchcraft in Great Britain. This marks the end of the witch trials for the country.

1519-1521 CE
Spain conquers the Aztecs. In the years following, the Mexican Inquisition brings many accused "witches" to trial. They are often Indigenous men and women, whose traditions are disrespected and misunderstood.

1783 CE
The Doruchów trials in Poland mark the last large witch trials in Europe.

1517 CE
The Protestant Reformation begins with Martin Luther. Religious turmoil fuels religious tension and fears around witchcraft.

1939 CE
The Wizard of Oz film is released. The costume and character of the Wicked Witch of the West would influence how witches were viewed over the next century.

1848 CE
Sisters Kate and Maggie Fox found the Spiritualist movement, which sweeps America and Europe. People use mediums to talk to the "spirits" of their loved ones.

1954 CE
Gerald Gardner, considered the founder of Wicca, publishes *Witchcraft Today*, the main book about Wicca.

15

MAGIC, RELIGION, and WITCHCRAFT

Throughout history, magic, religion, and witchcraft have been intertwined. However, most cultures have drawn key differences between the three, with each one meaning different things to different groups of people. So, what do they mean?

MAGIC

What is magic?
In the past, people didn't always separate magic, science, and religion. When we talk about magic today, we usually mean supernatural events or extraordinary powers that have no scientific explanation. It is hard to pin down one definition of magic, because what is magic for one person might be something quite different for another. Magic can be used for healing, creating protective charms, performing blessings, or cursing enemies.

Methods of magic
There are many ways of doing magic, from casting spells or curses and brewing potions, to predicting the future and talking to spirits. Some magic is used to cause harm, whereas other magic is used for good.

Who practices magic?
There are all sorts of people who use magic found throughout the myths, legends, and history of cultures all around the globe. Some of these people were real and some were made up. Examples include enchantresses, sorcerers, wizards, diviners, astrologers, necromancers, magicians, priests, conjurers, cunning folk, and of course ... witches!

RELIGION

What is religion?
Religion is the belief in and worship of supernatural powers or beings, such as gods or goddesses. Religions often have a set of rules or practices for believers to follow. Some cultures, especially in the ancient world, do not distinguish between magic and religion. Others, such as Christianity, consider them separate.

Gods and demons
Gods are supernatural beings that have power over humans and nature. Many religions also believe in demons—evil spirits who usually want to harm humans. Some cultures use magic to protect themselves from demons. Others worry that demons can be summoned by witches to do bad deeds.

Saints and miracles
A miracle is an amazing event that is believed by some religions to be caused by supernatural powers. In Christianity, miracles are often performed by special people who are believed to be chosen by God, called saints. Miracles might include healing illnesses or transforming one thing into another. A miracle isn't seen as magic by some religions, because it comes from God—but other people think it is magical.

WITCHCRAFT

What is witchcraft?
Witchcraft is the practice of magic. Throughout much of history, many cultures have believed that witchcraft was the practice of harmful magic through spells, charms, curses, potions, or summoning demons. Witches were thought to be evil people, who lived apart from society and wanted to cause trouble, and this book will help you understand why this was.

Modern witchcraft
Over time, witchcraft has come to mean many different things. Modern witches could be anyone who practices magic—good or bad. Witchcraft is sometimes linked to spiritual practices, such as healing rituals and meditation. It might be performed as part of a religion, or kept completely separate.

Chen Jinggu, China

1. The Morrigan
Ireland

The Morrigan is a famous goddess from Irish mythology who could shape-shift. She is associated with war, magic, and destiny.

2. Ceridwen
Wales

Ceridwen is an enchantress from Welsh mythology. She owned a magical cauldron and gave birth to the famous poet Taliesin.

3. Nicneven
Scotland

Nicneven is a witch or fairy queen found in Scottish folklore. She has powers over land and sea, and is served by a band of nymphs.

4. Circe
Greece

Circe is a beautiful sorceress from ancient Greek mythology. She would use her magic wand to turn men into pigs.

20. The Bell Witch
US

The Bell Witch is a legendary witch from Robertson County in Tennessee. Known as "Old Kate," her ghost was said to have haunted the family of John Bell in the early 19th century.

19. Soledad of Córdoba
Mexico

The legend of Soledad comes from Mexico. She was an herbalist who was imprisoned by the Mexican Inquisition, but used her magical powers to escape to freedom.

18. Pachamama
Andes Mountains

Pachamama is a goddess of the Indigenous people of the Andes Mountains in South America. She is an "Earth mother" who watches over the harvest and causes earthquakes.

LEGENDS AROUND the WORLD

Witches are found in the myths and legends of different cultures all around the world. They range from powerful goddesses to helpful enchantresses and dangerous demons. How many of these famous witch stories from around the globe have you heard?

Pachamama, Andes Mountains

17. Oya
Nigeria

Oya is a Nigerian Yoruba goddess, known as the "Great Mother of Witches." She can whip up storms and control water.

16. Yamauba
Japan

Yamauba are mountain witches who dwell in the peaks of Japan. They look like harmless old women, but are a danger to lost travelers.

15. Chen Jinggu
China

Chen Jinggu is a protective Chinese goddess of women and children. She trained as a Taoist priestess and rescued her people from drought and famine.

5. Grímhildr
Scandinavia

This evil sorceress is from Norse myth. She appears in the *Völsunga Saga*, and tricks the hero Sigurðr into marrying her daughter.

6. Louhi
Finland

Louhi is a powerful witch queen from Finnish mythology. She can shape-shift and appears in the epic *Kalevala* poem.

7. Melusine
France

Melusine is an enchantress from French legend with the upper body of a beautiful woman and the lower body of a fish.

8. La Befana
Italy

La Befana is a jolly old witch from Italian folklore who is said to deliver presents and sweets to children across Italy on Epiphany Eve.

La Befana, Italy

9. Jenny Greenteeth
England

Jenny Greenteeth is a witch from English folklore. She hides in rivers, waiting to pull victims into the water.

10. Baba Yaga
Russia and Ukraine

Baba Yaga is a witch from Eastern European folklore. She lives in a house that stands on chicken legs, and flies around the night sky in a mortar and pestle.

11. Medea
Georgia

Medea is a powerful witch from Colchis (modern Georgia). In Greek mythology, she fell in love with the hero Jason and helped him win the Golden Fleece.

12. Witch of Endor
Israel

This witch from Jewish tradition could talk to the dead. King Saul asked her to bring the spirit of the prophet Samuel, who then told him he was doomed.

14. Zhalmauyz Kempir
Kazakhstan

Zhalmauyz Kempir is a witch from the folk tales of Kazakhstan. She sometimes appears as an evil old woman and has many powers, from supernatural strength to shape-shifting and super speed.

13. Lilith
Iraq

This demon is from Jewish and Mesopotamian mythology. She is said to be the first wife of Adam, the first human, and is compared to the evil Mesopotamian demon Lamashtu, who terrorized women and children.

Lilith, Iraq

19

Chapter Two

ANCIENT ORIGINS

Witches, both real and imagined, are as old as the first civilizations in the world. Each ancient society had their own traditions and beliefs, and while not all ancient cultures believed in witches, most believed in magic or religion. These beliefs helped to shape the way people viewed magic and witches, and still impact how we see witches today. Read on to discover the ancient origins of witchcraft ...

ANCIENT SOURCES

How do we know so much about ancient magical beliefs? Most of our knowledge comes from the literature of different cultures, preserved across clay tablets, papyrus scrolls, books, and oral storytelling.

EGYPTIAN BOOK OF THE DEAD

The *Book of the Dead* is a text from ancient Egypt written on papyrus scrolls. It is commonly written in symbols called hieroglyphs, alongside beautiful illustrations. The book is made up of spells, which were thought to help a person make their way through the underworld to the afterlife.

THE TANAKH

The *Tanakh* is a Jewish religious text, also known in Hebrew as *Miqra*. It is made up of the Torah, the Nevi'im, and the Ketuvim. The *Tanakh* contains the story of the Witch of Endor—a sorceress who conjured up the spirit of the prophet Samuel for King Saul of Israel.

GREEK MAGICAL PAPYRI

The *Greek Magical Papyri* are a collection of papyrus scrolls found in Egypt. They date from around 100 BCE to 400 CE and contain a variety of spells, including love magic and instructions for creating magic amulets. The scrolls include ancient Greek, Egyptian, and Roman beliefs and rituals, helping us understand how these different cultures interacted with one another.

THE INDIAN ATHARVAVEDA

The *Atharvaveda* is one of four Vedas: sacred Hindu texts from ancient India, written around 1200 BCE. It contains hymns and spells for protection, healing, and success. Charms that promised long life to a loved one, or victory in battle, would have helped people feel less anxious in an uncertain world.

PICATRIX

Picatrix, or *Ghāyat al-Hakīm*, is an 11th-century spell book from Arabic Spain. The manuscript brings together ancient Arabic, Persian, and classical works on magic and astrology. Within its pages are spells for crafting talismans and instructions for rituals to master the power of the stars and planets.

THE POPOL VUH

Popol Vuh is an ancient Mayan manuscript that records the mythology and history of the K'iche' people. The text contains many stories, including the tale of the Hero Twins—Hunahpu and Xbalanque—who use magic to overcome a series of dangers and defeat the lords of the Mayan Underworld. The manuscript is especially important because records of Mesoamerican mythologies are rare since most of them were destroyed by invaders.

THE SACRED CORPUS OF IFÁ

Also known as *Odu Ifá*, the *Sacred Corpus of Ifá* is an ancient collection of divination texts. It was recorded orally by the Yoruba people of Nigeria and written down over many centuries. It is based on the teaching of Orunmila, a Yoruba sage, and the texts contain rituals, spells, and incantations to help make important decisions. A *Babalawo*, *Iyaláwo*, or *Ìyánifá*, which are different types of diviner, uses their knowledge of the system's signs and symbols to provide guidance.

MESOPOTAMIAN MAGIC

With a name meaning "between rivers," Mesopotamia (10,000-539 BCE) was a great region that stretched from the Tigris River to the Euphrates River, covering most of what is now Iraq—but its influence spread even further. Ancient Mesopotamia was home to some of the earliest civilizations in the world, including the Sumerians, the Akkadians, and the Babylonians.

WHAT DID MESOPOTAMIANS BELIEVE?

Mesopotamian people believed in a supernatural world where magic was everywhere, from the gods and goddesses they prayed to, to a lower order of demons that caused trouble. They thought magic could be used to harm or heal, and often blamed natural disasters on demons or witches. Seers, known as *baru*, predicted the future by observing the stars and interpreting omens.

WITCHES

Witches, known as *kaššapu* or *kaššaptu*, were feared figures in Mesopotamian culture. They could be men or women, but were more often depicted as female. People believed that witches could cause harm by casting curses. Sometimes they took small dolls or items that belonged to their victims and worked evil magic upon them in secret. They were mostly outcasts, but it is also likely that people visited local witches for help, perhaps in cursing their own enemies!

WITCH ENEMIES

The witches' opponents were magic-workers called *āšipu*. These religious figures served the gods, and spent years studying their craft from magical texts. *Āšipu* often worked alongside physical healers to cure the sick. Using charms and spells, they had the power to drive away demons and tame evil magic.

In this seal, an *āšipu* is shown wearing a cloak made of fish skin. The man beside him may be visiting the *āšipu* to be cured of an illness.

DISCOVERING HISTORY

Most of what we know about ancient Mesopotamia comes from clay tablets that archaeologists have found. Mesopotamians wrote on these tablets in a language called cuneiform, recording everything from shopping lists to epic stories. Thousands of clay tablets were stored in libraries. Some of these are known as the *Maqlû*, which means "burnings." The *Maqlû* tablets give instructions on how to deal with witches, and would have been used by *āšipu*.

Maqlû tablets provided instructions on how to tackle witchcraft by burning statuettes.

PROTECTING FROM HARM

The people of Mesopotamia protected themselves from harmful magic by taking part in religious rituals, praying to the gods, and wearing protective tokens, known as amulets. These amulets were often in the shape of the spirit they wanted to keep away, such as the plague demon Namtaru. They might also ask the *āšipu* for help if they thought they were being troubled by a witch.

This bronze plaque would have provided protection against the demons Lamashtu and Pazuzu.

EGYPTIAN MAGIC

In ancient Egypt, magic, known as *heka*, was part of everyday life, and was at the heart of people's beliefs about the world. There were no Egyptian "witches," but some people, such as priests and kings, were thought to have more control over magic than others. Magic was used to cure diseases, help crops grow, curse enemies, or help the dead pass on to the afterlife. The afterlife was very important to ancient Egyptians, because it was where they thought they would go when they died.

What is *Heka*?

Ancient Egyptians believed the creator god, Atum, used *heka* to create the universe. On Earth, powerful people such as kings and priests were able to use *heka*. The pharaoh was known as *hekau*, which means "possessor of magic." It was thought his very body held magic, so his hair and nail trimmings had to be disposed of carefully! Lector (reading) priests, known as *hery-heb*, were associated with magic, because the power of *heka* and the power of words were seen as the same. The magical rites they performed often involved reading a spell or incantation aloud, and performing an action, such as tying a knot or making an amulet.

Gods and *Heka*

All gods were thought to possess *heka*, but some were more powerful than others. Sekhmet, the lion goddess, was respected and feared for her magical gifts. It was believed that she had seven arrows that could bring plague and disease, and that she could set loose demons who would wreak havoc at the end of the year. To guard against them, magicians recited a special spell called *The Book of the Last Days of the Year*, and exchanged amulets in the shape of Sekhmet. The goddess Isis was also known as *Weret Hekau*, which means "Great Lady of Magic." After her husband Osiris was killed, she gathered his body parts and helped bring him back to life.

Ancient Egyptians believed that when they died, the gods would judge them.

Thoth, god of the moon, wisdom, and writing, was associated with magic. He was thought to have invented hieroglyphics.

DEATH AND MAGIC

For the ancient Egyptians, death was a very big deal. The rich would build elaborate tombs to house their dead, and the rituals of mummification—where the body was dried and wrapped in bandages—and burial took many days.

Scarab amulets gave the powers of life and regeneration to the dead.

Ankhs were thought to give eternal life.

The eye of Horus gave protection and the power of rebirth.

Ancient Egyptians would lay amulets on the dead to protect them on their journey to the afterlife.

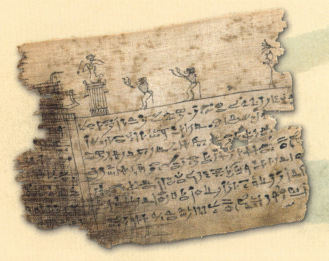

People were buried with extracts from books such as the *Book of the Dead* to guide and protect the soul. Sometimes spells were written on the walls of their tomb.

When a person died, their soul, known as *ba*, would travel to the afterlife. To do this, they had to pass a series of trials, or face a second death. To help them along this treacherous road, a person could use *heka*. When they came across dangers, such as demons, they could use magic words and gestures to defeat them.

HEAL OR HARM?

Magic and medicine went hand in hand in ancient Egypt, and spells and rituals were used alongside physical cures to treat patients. People thought that illness was caused by evil spirits, so priests would perform rituals to banish them—sometimes using foul-smelling ingredients such as dung.

As well as to heal, magic could also be used to harm. Curses were a common form of harmful magic. Names of enemies might be written on clay figures or pots, then trampled into the ground. Curses have been found written on the walls of tombs, warning off grave robbers and threatening them with dangerous animals.

Once a dead person had passed all the tests and was declared innocent, they became an *akh*, or spirit. They were then given magical powers of their own, which they could use to help their living relatives.

MUSLIMS and MAGIC

Islam is a major religion that began in present-day Saudi Arabia in the early 7th century, when the Prophet Muhammad began receiving messages from Allah (God). At this time, the people of the Arabian Peninsula lived in tribes and worshipped many different gods and goddesses. The Prophet Muhammad brought the word of Allah to the world, and the religion of Islam soon spread. The messages Allah gave to the Prophet Muhammad were written down in the Qur'an, a holy book for Muslims.

JINN

Jinn are shape-shifting spirits that are invisible to the human eye, but possess extraordinary powers. People believed in the Jinn long before Islam, but the Qur'an accepted them as Allah's creation, and they appear in many of its stories. Just like people, most Jinn are neither good nor bad, but capable of both. Some are known as *shayatin*, and these are dangerous demons to be feared.

SORCERY

The Qur'an considers magic harmful and forbids its use. The Arabic word for magic is *sihr*.

JINN ARE BEINGS OF SMOKELESS FLAME, IN THE SAME MANNER THAT HUMANS ARE SAID TO BE MADE OF EARTH.

THE STORY OF HARUT AND MARUT

Harut and Marut were two angels from Islamic mythology. Their story appears in the Qur'an.

One day, Harut and Marut began to complain to Allah that humans were always disobeying the word of God, but they were not being punished for their sins. Instead of getting angry, Allah challenged the angels to travel to Earth to see if they could resist the sins they ridiculed humans for committing.

"You may find," Allah said, "That you are no holier than the humans you judge!"

Sure enough, as soon as the angels found themselves on Earth, they were tempted to sin, and committed several crimes. One of these was teaching the arts of magic and sorcery to the people of Babylon, an ancient city in Mesopotamia. The angels were punished for their wrongdoing, but magical knowledge had now entered the world. The story is a warning tale for Muslims about the dangers of magic.

ASTROLOGY

Magic and sorcery are forbidden in the Qur'an. Pre-Islamic culture took great interest in practices such as divination and astrology. Astral magic (magic of the stars and planets) had a long history in many places around the world. Astrology flourished alongside this, and scholars were interested in drawing horoscopes and divining wisdom from the stars.

CHINESE MAGIC

Magic plays a rich role in Chinese history, and can be traced back thousands of years. Many elements of Chinese magic are linked to philosophy, religion, and cultural traditions that are still practiced today. In ancient China, some dynasties (families that ruled over the kingdom for generations) respected and admired people who practiced magic—however, this wasn't always the case.

Wu is an ancient Chinese term for sorcerer. Wu could be men or women, but in the late Zhou dynasty (about 1046-256 BCE), wu was most commonly used to mean a female sorceress. These women were thought to have amazing powers, such as the ability to heal people, fight evil spirits, tell the future, interpret dreams, and even summon rain.

There is also another Chinese word with the sound wu, which means "to dance." Movement was very important in the rituals of the wu, who were described as performing whirling dances, where they spoke to the spirits and made objects move through the air.

Wu is a Chinese term that means "sorcerer."

RAINMAKERS
In ancient China, droughts were common. There were periods when no rain fell, and the land grew dry and barren. To summon rain, the wu would perform rituals, asking for it to return and bless their crops. These rituals could be special dances, or ceremonies that used fire. Some wu performed these rituals freely, but others were forced to do them.

MAGIC AND DYNASTIES
During the Zhou dynasty, men and women became increasingly divided. Men believed they were more important than women. The wu, many of whom were women, came to be seen as a danger to society.

By the time of the Han dynasty (206 BCE-220 CE), witch hunts were taking place. Accusations of wu-gu (evil magic) began to spread throughout the court, and the punishment for such a crime was death. Even an empress found herself caught up in one such scandal. The once-respected wu now feared for their lives. Despite this, many stories exist of female wu who were turned into goddesses and worshipped.

CHEN JINGGU

The stories of the goddess Chen Jinggu have been passed down through Chinese legend. One story tells that Chen Jinggu was born from a drop of the goddess Guanyin's blood, and raised in the Chen family. Guanyin, the goddess of mercy and kindness, had promised to marry a man named Liu Qi. She created Chen Jinggu to marry him instead, but Chen Jinggu did not want to get married—she wanted to study Taoism, an ancient religious and philosophical tradition. To avoid marrying Liu Qi, she ran away to find refuge on Mount Lu, a place where the spirit and Earth worlds met.

After three years of study and training on Mount Lu, Chen Jinggu heard that her parents were being punished for her decision to avoid marriage. Despite warnings from her master, she left Mount Lu to return to her hometown. Chen Jinggu saved her parents and used the skills she had learned on Mount Lu to drive away demons. She even rescued Liu Qi from a snake demon, healing him with potions and talismans. Chen Jinggu married Liu Qi and became pregnant.

While she was pregnant, Chen Jinggu was unable to practice her magical rituals. During this time, a great drought came to the land, and the emperor demanded that the Taoist masters summon rain to help. Chen Jinggu performed a powerful spell to end the drought, saving the kingdom but sacrificing herself and her unborn child.

After her death, Chen Jinggu returned in spirit to Mount Lu to finish her studies. She became a protective goddess of women, children, and pregnancy, and is still worshipped across Asia today.

Empress Chen supposedly created POTIONS, performed SPELLS, and cast CURSES in order to get her husband back.

EMPRESS CHEN JIAO

2,000 years ago, China was ruled by the mighty Han dynasty (206 BCE–220 CE)–a royal family that oversaw a period of great wealth and success. It was also a time when fortunes could rise and fall like the turning of a wheel, as Empress Chen Jiao discovered, when she found herself accused of practicing dark magic and witchcraft.

Chen Jiao was born in 165 BCE. Her mother, Princess Guantao, was eager to arrange a good marriage for her daughter, so she began looking for a husband who was influential, and would provide the family with a positive social status. Her eyes soon fell upon the child prince, Liu Che.

Keen to bring the two young people together, Princess Guantao proposed the marriage to Emperor Jing, but he disapproved. Later, at a royal gathering, Prince Liu Che was asked who he might want as a wife. He rejected everyone until he spotted the lovely Chen Jiao, and boasted that he would "build a golden house for her." Emperor Jing believed that destiny had a plan, so he agreed to their engagement.

Years passed, and Liu Che eventually took the throne as the Emperor Wu and made Chen Jiao his empress. However, power and influence did not bring Chen Jiao happiness. Now her husband was emperor, she was expected to provide her husband with a son and heir to the throne. When no child arrived, Emperor Wu began having relationships with other women. Empress Chen Jiao was heartbroken.

> **THE EMPEROR DECLARED HE WOULD BUILD HER A GOLDEN HOUSE.**

Desperate to regain her husband's love, Chen Jiao resorted to magic. She was approached by a powerful sorceress named Chu Fu, who offered to help, despite witchcraft being illegal. The two women were said to have performed magical rituals day and night, drank potions, and slept together in one bed.

However, the empress's relationship with Chu Fu was soon discovered, and the scandal rocked the empire. Chu Fu was executed for practicing dark magic, along with around three hundred others who were thought to practice sorcery. Chen Jiao was removed from her position as empress and sent into exile in disgrace. Chen Jiao lived out the rest of her life under house arrest at Long Gate Palace, grieving for her lost husband.

JAPANESE MAGIC

Magic has always been an important part of Japanese culture, and is strongly tied to religion and folklore. Japan's traditional religion, Shinto, teaches that everything—from rivers to mountains—is home to *kami*. *Kami* are spirits whose powers can be controlled by people with special knowledge. Although they are not "witches," there are many different spirits in Japanese folklore, some who might help you, and some who might harm you.

MAGIC IN JAPAN

Onmyōdō is a divination practice based on the powers of yin-yang and the five elements: wood, fire, earth, metal, and water. People who practiced *onmyōdō* told fortunes, read omens from the stars, and carried out exorcisms. Their predictions were used to make important royal decisions, until they were banned by Emperor Meiji in 1868.

YŌKAI

Yōkai are shape-shifting supernatural spirits from Japanese folklore. They come in many forms and can be good or evil. One type of *yōkai* are *yamauba*—"mountain hags" who live deep in mountains and forests, and feed on lost wanderers. Legend tells that they were once human, but were turned into monsters after being driven from their communities.

KITSUNE

The *kitsune* are fox spirits. They are a type of *yōkai* that can be good or mischievous. As *kitsune* age, they become more powerful and grow more tails—as many as nine! It is thought that "fox witches" can command *kitsune* by making deals with them. They might ask for magical favors, but could also be possessed by the *kitsune*.

BAKENEKO

The *bakeneko*, another type of *yōkai*, is a supernatural cat. *Bakeneko* have many magical abilities, such as dancing, possessing people, and casting curses. They were thought to lick lamp oil, which was said to be an omen of strange events to come. This might be because people used to burn cheap fish oil in lamps, which tasted delicious to cats!

THE CAT WITCH OF OKAZAKI

Late one day, three travelers were on their way home from a pilgrimage. The road had been long, and they were tired and hungry, so they decided to stop at a temple for a rest. They were welcomed into the temple by a kind woman, who told them her name was Osan, and said they could spend the night. Grateful, they accepted her offer. However, things soon took a peculiar turn.

During the evening, the travelers noticed two cats dancing on their hind legs. Osan reassured them that there was no need to worry—this was perfectly normal. Later that night, one of the travelers glanced up at the wall and spotted a very strange sight—something was wrong with Osan's shadow. Instead of an old lady, it was the shadow of an enormous cat. The traveler suddenly realized that Osan was a *bakeneko*, and that he was in great danger. He fled the temple, relieved to have made it out alive ...

... but his two friends were not so lucky.

GREEK MAGIC

Like in many ancient societies, magic played an essential role in ancient Greece. Belief in the supernatural was part of everyday life—from the workings of the gods to the rising of the moon. While practicing religion and prayer was public, people often turned to private magic for protection, healing, and cursing. Amulets, charms, potions, and spells were common methods of wielding magic to your advantage.

ORACLES

Ancient Greeks often looked to the gods for wisdom and guidance, and the best way to ask them a question was through an oracle. Oracles were people who the gods spoke through. They were usually women who lived away from society in a sacred place. The most famous was Pythia, the Oracle of Delphi, who claimed to speak for Apollo and gave prophecies.

ENCHANTRESSES

The witches of ancient Greece are creatures of myth and magic. Generally described as young and beautiful, they are as enchanting as they are dangerous: from Circe, a mysterious, but powerful sorceress, to Medea, an expert in brewing powerful potions. The poet Theocritus wrote about a young witch called Simaetha, who was abandoned by her lover, Delphis. Simaetha cast a binding spell and called upon the moon to help her enchant Delphis back.

HECATE

Hecate was a powerful ancient Greek goddess associated with the moon, magic, and witchcraft. She is often depicted as a triple goddess, with three bodies facing in different directions to represent her influence over the three spheres: Earth, Ocean, and the Underworld. It was said that "her powers extended far beyond the realms of the heavens, earth, and seas." Even Zeus, king of the gods, honored and respected her.

As a goddess of magic and the Underworld, people who practiced magic would pray to her for assistance. People would leave curse tablets at Hecate's shrines, begging her to take revenge on their enemies. However, Hecate had a strong sense of justice—if you asked for her help, you had to be sure your reasons were fair!

As fierce as she was, Hecate could also be a force for good. One myth tells of how Hecate saw the god Hades taking Persephone to the Underworld, and helped Persephone's desperate mother search for her. In another tale, Hecate helped Hecuba, queen of Troy, escape her enemies by turning her into a great black dog. It was said that, after that, dogs always howled when Hecate was near, and were considered her sacred companions.

HER POWERS EXTENDED FAR BEYOND THE REALMS OF THE HEAVENS, EARTH, AND SEAS.

CIRCE

Daughter of the sun god Helios and the ocean nymph Perse, Circe was a powerful goddess in Greek mythology, dreamt up by Greek poets. She was known for her bewitching voice and her skills with potions, which she mixed in an elegant golden bowl.

Circe lived on Aeaea, a wild and wooded island. Her beautiful palace was guarded by men who she had transformed into wolves and mountain lions.

CIRCE AND ODYSSEUS

One of the best-known stories about Circe tells of her encounter with Odysseus, the king of Ithaca. The story comes from an ancient Greek poem called the *Odyssey*.

Odysseus was known for being clever, but met his match in Circe. After narrowly escaping some Laestrygonians (man-eating giants), Odysseus and his men found themselves washed up on the shores of Aeaea. The men soon grew hungry, so they decided to split up to search for food. Odysseus led one group, while his brave soldier Eurylochus led the other, heading deep into the woods.

They came across Circe's palace, nestled among the trees. Fearsome mountain lions and wolves lounged in the doorway, but the men couldn't resist the sweet voice inviting them inside.

Suspecting it was a trap, Eurylochus refused to enter, and watched silently from the shadows instead.

Inside, Circe welcomed the men, offering food and wine to drink. They accepted greedily, not realizing that she had enchanted the feast with magical drugs. When the men finished their meal, Circe tapped them with her wand, transforming them into pigs. Horrified, Eurylochus ran back to the shore to tell Odysseus.

Odysseus immediately set off to confront Circe. Suddenly, a stranger appeared before him—the messenger god, Hermes. He knew of Circe's powers, and offered Odysseus a plant with black roots and white flowers, which he called moly. Carrying this, he said, would make Odysseus immune to Circe's spells.

When Odysseus arrived at Circe's palace, she served him delicious food and wine. Once he had finished, Circe raised her magic wand and struck him. However, thanks to Hermes's gift, the spell didn't work. Instead, Odysseus leapt to his feet and pointed his sword at the enchantress.

Impressed by the king's bravery, Circe promised to release his men from the spell. Odysseus admired Circe's skill and power, and the two became friends. Odysseus and his men lived on Aeaea for almost a year, before setting off for Ithaca. When they left, Circe offered the men advice and guidance for their journey home.

Circe could use potions and spells to turn humans into LIONS, WOLVES, and PIGS.

ROMAN MAGIC

Ancient Roman society was very concerned about harmful magic—in one of their early sets of laws, the Twelve Tables, the use of incantations for evil is forbidden. Despite this, magic played a large role in everyday life, from protective charms to healing herbs. While male sorcerers were respected, harmful magic was associated with women, and witches were feared for their power.

OLD, FRIGHTENING, AND POWERFUL

While witches in ancient Greece were thought of as young and beautiful, ancient Roman witches were often shown as spiteful old women, whose magic was dark, dangerous, and immensely powerful. Some stories tell of the *strix*, a fearsome owl-shaped demon, who would terrorize households during the night. It was thought that some witches could transform into *strixes*.

CURSE TABLETS

These items were popular methods of magic in both ancient Greece and ancient Rome. Written on thin pieces of lead, curse tablets would ask certain gods and goddesses to carry out revenge. About 1,600 curse tablets have been found, including a large horde in the Roman spa town of Bath, England. The curses range from funny to downright gruesome. Some hope that their victims' jokes will fall flat, while others wish that a love rival will be "dissolved into liquid."

Ancient curse tablet

EVERYDAY MAGIC

For most people in ancient Rome, magic was found in even the smallest of everyday actions. People would hang charms and amulets outside homes or carry them around in the folds of their togas. People sick with love might seek out love potions from skilled herbalists, who were respected for their healing powers. Even children would wear either a *bulla* or a *lunula*—a protective amulet worn around their neck to guard them against the evil eye.

MAGICAL PLANTS

Plants are powerful! Humans throughout history have known that some plants can heal or harm. The ancient Greeks called magic that used herbs, potions, or drugs *pharmakeia*. There were many poisonous plants that were associated with witches, some of which are shown on this page.

Deadly nightshade

As well as being very poisonous, deadly nightshade can cause hallucinations, making it a popular ingredient for witches to use. Although it was dangerous, medieval women sometimes put drops of deadly nightshade into their eyes to make them shine! A substance called atropine, which comes from the plant, is still used in medicine today.

Vervain

Also known as "the Enchanter's herb," vervain was linked to ancient magical and religious practices. Ancient Egyptians believed it came from the tears of the goddess Isis, and Christians thought it was used to treat Jesus's wounds when he was on the cross. Because of this, vervain was a key ingredient in protective spells, and was used to cleanse sacred spaces.

Datura
Native to North and Central America, datura is known for its beautiful trumpet-shaped flowers. It has been used for both magical ceremonies and religious purposes for hundreds of years. When rubbed into the skin, it causes hallucinations, helping users enter a dreamlike trance. Datura is commonly called "hell's bells" or "Devil's snare."

Mugwort
Sometimes called "the mother of herbs," mugwort has been used in magic and medicine for thousands of years, especially for treating women's illnesses. In many places around the world, it is drunk as a tea or used as an ingredient in recipes.

Henbane
This plant is associated with magical practices due to its ability to cause powerful hallucinations. When rubbed on the skin, it was said to make people feel like they were flying. People thought that witches made ointments from henbane to allow them to fly to their secret meetings. In large doses henbane can be deadly.

Wormwood
Mugwort and wormwood are both part of the same family. Wormwood has been used for centuries to treat issues with the stomach and intestines.

Ginseng
Ginseng has been a popular ingredient in traditional Korean, Chinese, and Japanese herbal medicines for thousands of years. Ginseng is still widely used today, because modern research has shown it can help strengthen the immune system and prevent tiredness. You might find ginseng in traditional remedies and herbal teas.

HOODOO HOT FOOT POWDER

Hot foot powder is used by practitioners of Hoodoo (an African-American folk religion) to ward off unwanted people or attention. The powder is usually made of minerals, herbs, and spices, including salt, pepper, and chili flakes. The ingredients are ground up and placed somewhere the target will walk, or even directly inside their shoes! Hot foot powder does not harm its victims, it simply encourages them to leave an area or person alone.

A binding spell can be cast by tying a doll of a person up in string.

BINDING MAGIC

Some curses involve a type of magic called binding magic. Binding spells are cast upon a person to "bind them up," perhaps to stop them from winning a sporting event or triumphing in a court of law.

There are several ways to cast a binding spell. A popular choice is to make a doll of the person being cursed, which can then be bound in string or cord. In the ancient world, binding was also used in love spells, but this was dark magic. Such spells often threatened pain to the beloved if they did not return the spell caster's feelings!

CURSES

What is a curse? A curse is a wish or a spell of misfortune, intended to bring harm to one or more people. It may be short-lived or follow families through many generations. Breaking a curse often involves using counter-magic, usually through rituals or prayers. Throughout history, people thought witches used dark magic to lay curses on people and animals.

EVIL EYE

The evil eye is a curse brought about by looking at someone with envy or evil intention. Belief in the evil eye has existed since prehistory, and is found in many cultures around the globe. The evil eye is thought to bring harm and misfortune to those it lands upon. People who have attracted success, beauty, and status are also more likely to attract the evil eye.

Different cultures have their own ways of protecting against the evil eye, using a mix of charms, amulets, and protective gestures. The *hamsa*, also known as the hand of Fatima, is a hand-shaped amulet that is a popular charm in West Asian and North African countries. In the Balkans and West Asia, blue and white beads known as *nazar* are thought to ward off the evil eye by reflecting its gaze away. Caribbean families often guard their houses with blue ornaments, while Senegalese people wear cowrie shell bracelets to absorb the evil eye's energy.

Nazar

The hamsa, or hand of Fatima

NOROI

Noroi is the Japanese term for a curse, a hex, or bad fortune. This curse might be brought about on purpose or by accident.

One ritual to cast a curse is called *Ushi no toki mairi*. The rite must take place between 1 a.m. and 3 a.m., known as the hours of the Ox. The curser hammers nails or a straw doll of their victim into a sacred tree at a Shinto shrine. This is repeated seven days in a row, but if anyone catches them in the act, it will not work.

One of the earliest records of *Noroi* is the 75th emperor of Japan, Emperor Sutoku, who gave up the throne and spent time copying beautiful scriptures. He wanted to present them at court, but people worried that they might be cursed, so refused him. After he died, Sutoku is believed to have transformed into an *onryō*—a spirit who wanted revenge. He was said to haunt the empire from then on.

45

MEDEA

Medea was a princess and powerful sorceress in Greek mythology. She was the daughter of King Aeetes of Colchis, and the niece of Circe, a feared enchantress. Like her aunt, Medea had a gift for magic and was skilled at making potions. She is best known for her love affair with the Greek hero Jason, but Medea's story ends in tragedy.

When Medea was a young woman, a man named Jason came to her home. Son of Aeson, the rightful king of Iolcus, Jason had come looking for the Golden Fleece—a legendary fleece that was said to have magical properties. Jason's uncle, King Pelias, had seized the kingdom of Iolcus, but agreed to give up the throne in exchange for the fleece. Determined to claim the throne that was rightfully his, Jason gathered a band of heroes and set sail in his ship, the *Argo*, to find the fleece.

The Golden Fleece belonged to Medea's father. When Jason asked King Aeetes for the fleece, the king demanded that Jason first complete a series of dangerous challenges. Luckily for Jason, he had the support of three powerful goddesses: Hera, Athena, and Aphrodite. To help him, they asked Eros, the god of love, to fire an arrow at Medea, so she would fall in love with Jason.

From the first moment Medea saw Jason, she knew she would do anything to keep him safe. Ignoring her father's instructions not to help the hero, she decided to assist Jason with his challenges.

The Challenges

Jason's first task was to plow a field with fire-breathing oxen. Using her skill with herbs and potions, Medea made an ointment that protected Jason from the oxen's fire. Next, he had to sow the field with dragon's teeth. She warned him that they would turn into soldiers and gave him instructions on how to defeat them.

When Jason succeeded in completing these first tasks, Medea knew her father would realize she had disobeyed him. She decided to run away, and escaped to the *Argo* with Jason, who promised to marry her. But, before they

could leave, there was one final challenge to face—taking the Golden Fleece. The fleece was guarded by a fearsome dragon, who never slept. Jason didn't know how to defeat it, and once again relied upon Medea's skills and bravery.

A Mighty Enchantress

Medea was a woman of great power, who did not always use her magical abilities for good. She carried out terrible acts of violence when she was wronged—like how many witches have been portrayed throughout history.

However, Medea was a complicated anti-hero. Alongside her ability to cause great harm, she also had the ability to protect and heal. After helping Jason collect the Golden Fleece, she cured the Greek hero Hercules of his madness, and helped King Aegeus to have children. It is no wonder that this complex enchantress has inspired many works of art and literature.

Before the dragon could harm them, Medea began to sing a soothing song. She approached the dragon and blew magical herbs into its eyes, making it fall into a deep sleep. Medea and Jason grabbed the fleece and escaped, setting off for Jason's homeland of Greece. Throughout the journey, Medea did everything she could to protect Jason—she was even responsible for the deaths of the many people who got in their way, including that of King Pelias and her own brother.

Betrayal

For a while, Jason and Medea lived happily in Corinth with their two sons. But Medea was a foreigner, and Jason thought it would be better for him to marry a Greek princess instead. Despite his promise to Medea and everything she had done for him, he abandoned her. Heartbroken and filled with rage, she sent his new bride a poisoned cloak as a wedding present, killed the children she shared with Jason, and rode off in a chariot pulled by dragons.

Aphrodite's herb
Oregano is a common herb used in cooking. The ancient Greeks believed it to be a favorite of Aphrodite. Oregano has traditionally been used in love potions, spells, and protective charms against unwanted attention.

Love-in-idleness
The wild pansy, also known as "love-in-idleness," is a flower linked to love in Greek and Roman mythology. It was said to have been shot by one of Cupid's arrows, giving it aphrodisiac properties. In Shakespeare's play *A Midsummer Night's Dream*, a potion is made using its petals.

Japanese lotus root
In medieval Japan, people used many unusual ingredients to create potions, from eels and charred newts to lotus roots. The lotus flower is seen as a symbol of purity and enlightenment in Japan today.

LOVE SPELLS and POTIONS

People around the world, from ancient Greece to African kingdoms, have always been drawn to spells and potions that cause others to have feelings for them. A potion or ingredient that does this is known as an aphrodisiac, after Aphrodite—the Greek goddess of love. However, love potions are often more disturbing than their name suggests, causing their victims to be controlled in a sometimes sinister way.

Minthe's mixture
In Greek mythology, the nymph Minthe was in love with the king of the Underworld, Hades. When Hades' wife Persephone found out, she was furious and turned Minthe into a plant, which we now call spearmint. Hades softened the spell by making the leaves smell nice. Spearmint has been linked to love and compassion ever since.

Medieval mandrake
The mandrake is a curious plant. Its roots are thought to look like a small human, and people even believed that it would scream when pulled from the ground, as if it were alive! The fruits of the mandrake are known as "apples of love" and have been used in potions from ancient through to medieval times.

Thorn apple
The datura plant, also known as "thorn apple," was known to be a magical ingredient in witches' brews. Across India, it has been used as a common ingredient in love potions. One recipe asks for "ten datura seeds, peppercorns, and one long pepper" to be "crushed and mixed with honey." However, the datura plant is poisonous, and should be handled with care.

"Charming" love spells
Love spells have been found written in ancient Greek and preserved on papyrus scrolls from 4th-century Egypt. Spells often promised the user eternal love, however some were more sinister, aiming to "bind" a loved one to another forever, and to cause suffering if they were apart.

THE DEATH OF HERCULES

Hercules (also known as Heracles) was a Greek hero, famous for carrying out his Twelve Labors—12 challenging tasks set by his king. However, his life ended in tragedy.

Deianira, Hercules's wife, adored him, and he loved her in return. One day, a centaur appeared and tried to steal Deianira away. Outraged, Hercules shot the centaur with a special arrow—it had been dipped in the poisonous blood of the Hydra, which was deadly to any who touched it.

As the centaur lay dying, he gave Deianira his blood-soaked tunic. "Give this to your husband to wear," he said, "and he will love only you, forever." Deianira took the tunic and hid it away. Years later, she found out that Hercules had fallen in love with a beautiful princess.

Upset and jealous, she wondered how to bring her husband back to her. Then, she remembered the centaur's tunic. Hoping to make Hercules love her again, she gave him the tunic to wear.

But it was a trick! The blood of the Hydra, though old, was still deadly. Instead of reuniting her with her husband, Deianira realized that she had instead lost him forever—the great hero was dying. With the last of his strength, Hercules built his own funeral pyre, and climbed up onto it. Deianira wept, and cursed the day she had believed the sly centaur.

49

Chapter Three

RELIGION, MYTHS, and MAGIC

After the era of ancient civilizations came the medieval period, which lasted from about 500 to 1500 CE. This was a time that saw the rise of new empires and kingdoms, when religious ideas were shared, knowledge of science and mathematics spread, and people believed in myths and magic. Many people used witches and magic to explain the world around them, but many others feared things they didn't understand, and fought against the idea of "magic."

WHAT IS THE MEDIEVAL PERIOD?

The medieval period took place between about 500 and 1500 CE, and saw the world change beyond recognition. In Europe and Western Asia, the end of the Roman Empire led to new empires and kingdoms. People migrated across Europe, bringing their beliefs with them, and older religions were gradually replaced by newer ones such as Christianity and Islam. It was a time of learning and discovery, when universities were invented.

The MEDIEVAL MIND

Magic played a complicated role in medieval Europe. It was condemned by the Christian Church, but helpful magic, such as healing spells or folk charms, was generally accepted. In other parts of the world, people had less clear relationships with magic: for African, Indigenous American, and Asian cultures, sorcerers could be seen as good or bad.

THE MEDIEVAL MIND AND MAGIC

For medieval Europeans, the world was full of mystery. Science and magic were not separate, and strange events were often labeled as supernatural. But the spread of Christianity changed people's attitudes, because magic was thought to go against Christian beliefs. Islam and Judaism also disapproved, though magic was still practiced in some forms.

ASTROLOGY

Astrology is the belief that the moon, sun, stars, and planets can affect people and nature. In medieval Arab societies, the astrolabe, an instrument created using astronomical calculations, could be used to find the direction of Mecca and the right time for prayers. It was also used for astrology, such as casting horoscopes. The Mayan peoples of Mexico could also read the skies. They created sophisticated calendars using astronomy, and believed that the sun and moon were gods.

MEDICAL MAGIC

During the medieval period, magic and medicine were not separate: people happily combined healing medicine with charms and spells. The 11th-century *Leechbook* mixed herbal remedies with religious charms. People believed that relics (the remains of saints) had healing properties, and monarchs were blessed with the power to cure illness.

DARK SORCERY

Despite the acceptance of medical magic or protective charms, some arts were strictly off limits. In particular, people feared necromancy—magic of the dead that involved summoning spirits to tell the future, bringing someone back to life, or using the dead as weapons. Although necromancers argued they were merely using God's power, they were suspected of communicating with demons.

MEDIEVAL JEWISH MAGIC

Magic was condemned in Judaism, but was still practiced by people at all levels of society. In medieval Jewish magic, words held great power: it was believed that the right words could banish demons or raise the dead. They could also create a *golem*—a creature made from clay and brought to life. Christians sometimes accused Jewish people of dark magic and used it as an excuse for violence against them.

EUROPEAN WITCHES

Fictional stories of witches are found in the folklore and fairy tales of many European countries. Sometimes they are wicked old women, and other times they are powerful goddesses. Many of their stories were told to frighten children into behaving themselves, and are still popular today.

Frau Perchta
This alpine goddess of winter in Germany, Austria, and Slovenia is sometimes described as the "Great Goddess of the North." She has two forms: an old wrinkled hag and a beautiful young woman. At Christmastime she is said to visit homes to make sure that the household chores have been done, and people make offerings of food to please her.

Baba Yaga
A character from Slavic folklore, Baba Yaga is an old woman who lives deep in the forest in a hut that stands on chicken legs. When she travels, she flies around in a wooden mortar and pestle. In some stories, Baba Yaga is fearsome and wicked, known for preying on innocent children. In other tales, she is kind and wise, helping the hero or heroine.

La Befana
This friendly witch appears in Italian folklore. On Epiphany Eve (January 5), she flies through the night on a broomstick, delivering gifts to children. She is usually pictured as a jolly old woman, covered in soot from flying up and down chimneys. People leave out wine and food for La Befana and, in return, she may sweep their house clean!

Lutzelfrau
This witch is found in German, Slovenian, and Croatian folklore, and is thought to fly through the skies at night followed by a band of goblins. On St. Lucy's Day (December 13), Lutzelfrau is believed to visit children. If they have been good, she gives them gifts of apples, nuts, and dried plums.

NORSE MAGIC

Before Christianity was introduced, the Norse peoples of Scandinavia had their own rich and fascinating belief system. In Norse mythology, Earth (known as Midgard) was one of nine worlds, all connected by an ash tree called Yggdrasil. There are two sets of gods, the *Aesir* and the *Vanir*, but Norse mythology is full of other magical creatures, such as dwarves, dragons, witches, and elves.

SEIDHR

The Norse people lived approximately 1,200 years ago, and believed in many kinds of magic. The Norse word for sorcery was *seidhr*, and it was used to predict and shape the future. Practicing *seidhr* might involve visiting the spirit world, chanting, or reciting spells. It was mainly done by women, because it was seen as shameful or embarrassing for men to practice it.

THE VÖLVA AND THE NORNS

The *Völva* were powerful women who were experts in the art of *seidhr*. They used wands or staffs when practicing their craft, and it was said that they could change the path of fate, as well as cast love spells, raise storms, and shape-shift into different forms.

The *Norns*, Norse goddesses of fate, lived by a well beneath Yggdrasil and spent their days watering the tree and spinning out the threads of life. They were more powerful than the gods, because they controlled destiny.

FREYJA

Freyja was a powerful Norse goddess of love, magic, and war. She was a member of the *Vanir*, the gods who rule in Vanaheim. Freyja was skilled in the art of *seidhr*, and supposedly taught the practice to Odin, king of the gods, who was insulted for practicing it. She traveled in a chariot pulled by giant cats, and wore a cloak of falcon feathers, as well as *Brisingamen*—a necklace crafted by dwarves. It is said that after a battle, half of the fallen warriors go to Odin's hall, Valhalla. The other half are taken to *Fólkvangr*, a meadow realm ruled over by Freyja.

Freyja was one of the most popular goddesses, and was worshipped all across the Viking world. She was known for her cleverness, her beauty, and her ability to shape-shift. Some stories say that when she wept, her tears turned into amber and gold. People were always watching for signs from the gods, and just as ravens were believed to be messengers of Odin, a black cat crossing your path meant that Freyja was watching you!

57

FAIRY TALES and FOLKLORE

Witches appear in folklore and fairy tales from all around the globe. Fairy tales were particularly popular in Europe during the 1800s, when people such as the Brothers Grimm published collections of old stories. The tales were told to both children and adults, and were filled with magic and wonder. The witch takes many forms in such stories, but she is almost always the villain!

WITCH IN THE WOODS

A common theme in fairy tales and folklore is the witch in the woods. People wondered who or what might be lurking in forests, so scary stories helped discourage children from wandering too far from home. One tale, *Hansel and Gretel*, tells of a brother and sister who get lost in the woods and are captured by a witch living in a house made of gingerbread and candy!

La Xtabay

La Xtabay is a beautiful but monstrous demon from Mayan mythology. She lives deep in the woods of Mexico, Belize, and Guatemala, and lures men into the darkness. Once she has trapped them, she transforms into a serpent and eats them whole!

Dzunukwa

The Kwakwaka'wakw people of British Columbia, Canada, tell stories of Dzunukwa–an old hag who dwells between the trunks of cedar trees and preys on the young. Children are warned not to follow the "hu" sound of the wind through the forest because it is the call of Dzunukwa!

THE WITCH AS MOTHER

In some fairy tales, the witch is given the role of a mother, but she is usually portrayed as an evil stepmother—the opposite of what a good mother was expected to be. These tales were popular at a time when people did not live as long and remarrying was common, so they might have reflected real fears people had about family.

THE ELEMENTAL WITCH

Some fictional witches are strongly tied to the elements, including the Sea Witch and the Snow Queen, who appear in the fairy tales of the Danish author Hans Christian Andersen.

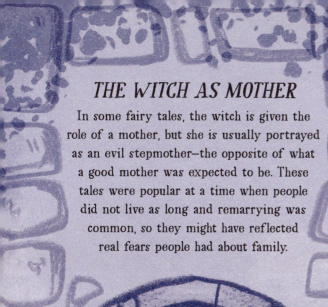

Snow White

In the tale of *Snow White*, little Snow White's mother dies and her father marries again. His new wife is young, beautiful, and a witch. Every day she looks into her magic mirror, asking it: "Who is the fairest of them all?" One day, the mirror replies: "Snow White." Mad with jealousy, the witch tries to kill her stepdaughter using a ribbon, an enchanted comb, and a poisoned apple.

The Snow Queen

In *The Snow Queen*, an evil witch queen rules over a land of snow and ice. She kidnaps a young boy and takes him to her palace. His brave friend faces many dangers to rescue him, and her love and friendship melt the spell he is under. *The Snow Queen* may have inspired C. S. Lewis's *The Lion, The Witch, and The Wardrobe*, the tale of a witch who has taken over the country of Narnia. She keeps it in everlasting winter and wins over children with her magic.

CREATURES of the NIGHT

Have you ever wondered what creatures could be lurking in the shadows of night? Stories of creatures who dwell in darkness can be found throughout history and around the globe. Different cultures have their own folklore, but there are some similarities to be found between them.

Strix

The *strix* is a creature from ancient Roman folklore. Believed to be bad luck, the *strix* took the form of a large bird with gray wings and sharp claws. It was thought to come out at night and feed on the blood of humans. In some stories, the *strix* was a person who transformed into this terrible bird to do evil. Perhaps because of this, the Romans also used the word *strix* to mean witch.

Manananggal

A legendary creature from the Philippines, the *manananggal* is a monstrous female creature, who can separate the two halves of its body. Although she appears as a beautiful woman during the day, at night she grows batlike wings and flies through the air. Some Filipino families place salt and garlic around their homes to protect themselves against the *manananggal*.

THE NIGHT AND MAGIC

The night has always seemed magical, and many myths and legends tell of spells or rituals taking place under the cloak of darkness. Witches and other supernatural creatures were thought to be at their strongest at night. That's why the hour after midnight is still called "the witching hour." In European folklore, night was a time for secret meetings, and people believed that witches would gather in their covens to perform magic after dark.

Lamia

This female demon from Greek mythology was once a beautiful woman, but was cursed by the goddess Hera to be a monster with a thirst for blood. Half-woman, half-snake, she would sit in the grass and wait for victims. Just like the *strix*, the word *lamia* has sometimes been used to mean witch.

Tlahuelpuchi

These creatures of the night can be found in the folklore of the Mexican state Tlaxcala, and come from the stories of the Nahua culture. The *tlahuelpuchi* are humans by day, but at night they shape-shift, often into the form of a turkey, to go hunting. They are born with this curse and can use their powers once they are teenagers. According to legend, they even glow in the dark.

Vampire

Many creatures of the night share similarities with vampires. Vampire legends have been popular all around the globe for hundreds of years, but particularly in Eastern Europe. Vampires were thought to rise from the dead to drink human blood. They had pale skin, sharp teeth, and couldn't be seen in mirrors. One of the most famous vampire stories is Bram Stoker's horror novel *Dracula*.

PROTECTIVE CHARMS

Apotropaic means "to turn away." Apotropaic magic, or protective magic, is magic used to ward off harm and misfortune. For thousands of years, cultures all over the world have used different forms of apotropaic magic to protect themselves, from wearing precious amulets to writing special incantations.

Amulets

An amulet is a special object that is believed to protect its owner from negative energy. Amulets have been used for thousands of years. In ancient Mesopotamia, they were carved into the shapes of demons that people wanted to frighten away. Ancient Egyptian amulets were made from precious stones and buried with their owners to protect them in the afterlife. Jade amulets played an important role in Chinese culture, while Norse peoples wore the symbol of Thor's hammer—called the Mjölnir—to ward off evil.

Witch marks

Symbols known as witch marks were scratched into buildings to provide protection for those who lived there. It was common to place witch marks above windows, doorways, and fireplaces, because people believed this was where witches, demons, or evil spirits might try to enter their homes. Witch marks have even been found on furniture, gravestones, and inside caves. There are lots of different kinds of protective marks, from diagonal lines and crosses, to mazes and daisy wheels (also known as hexafoils).

Concealed shoes

In early modern England, people believed that hiding shoes in your home would act as a protective charm. Like witch marks, shoes would be hidden in "weak" spots around the house, such as inside a chimney, under a window, or even in the roof. It isn't known why shoes were chosen, but it's possible that some people believed any bad spirits trying to enter the home would become trapped in them! This practice continued until at least the 19th century.

Mythical symbology

In ancient Greece and Rome, certain symbols were thought to provide powerful protection against harm. The Gorgons were fearsome snake-haired creatures from Greco-Roman mythology. People believed a gorgon's head could ward off evil, so they would use it as a symbol of protection on their armor, shields, and entryways.

Modern superstitions

From throwing spilled salt over your left shoulder to avoiding stepping on cracks in the pavement, we still look for ways to protect ourselves against bad luck! Even today, four-leaf clovers are considered a lucky symbol—a belief which began in the ancient Celtic world, when druids would carry them to ward off evil spirits.

Incantation bowls

Also known as "demon bowls," incantation bowls are found throughout West Asia, and were popular during the 6th to 8th centuries. Prayers, psalms, or requests for protection from evil were written in a spiral inside a bowl, beginning at the edge and moving toward the center. The bowls were then buried upside down at the boundary of a building or room in order to trap evil spirits who tried to enter.

63

Rowan trees
The rowan is a tree with feathery green leaves and deep red berries. Its wood was thought to provide powerful protection against witchcraft, and would often be carried as a charm. Rowan sprigs would be bent into the shape of crosses, and tied onto cattle to keep them safe.

GROWING MAGIC

Pumpkins
An iconic symbol of witchcraft, carving faces into pumpkins was thought to keep away evil spirits on All Hallows' Eve, also known as Halloween. This is a tradition that began with turnips in Celtic nations. In the religion of Santería, pumpkins are associated with the deity Oshun.

Plants are amazing. They have played a vital role in medicine, cooking, and crafts for thousands of years. But is there more to them than meets the eye? The myths and legends of cultures around the globe prove that people have long believed in the magical power of nature. From protection against witchcraft to driving away evil spirits, the natural world has inspired endless supernatural beliefs.

Hazel trees

The hazel is a tree that bears yellow catkins in winter and delicious nuts in the fall. Some people believed that a cross made from hazel would protect against witches. In one Irish myth, a salmon gained all the wisdom in the world when it ate nine hazelnuts that had fallen into the sacred Well of Segais.

Blackthorn trees

Found at the edges of woodland, blackthorn trees produce white flowers in the spring, followed by sloe berries in the fall. They have a sinister reputation in folklore, because people thought witches used the thorned branches for wands or for pricking their victims. In Celtic mythology, it is said that the blackthorn tree provides a home for fairies.

Xiaojun mushrooms

People have believed that xiaojun mushrooms, also known as "laughing gyms" or "petticoat mottlegills," possessed magical properties. The shamans of Yue in southern China would collect them to use in their rituals. Eating these mushrooms could cause people to laugh uncontrollably, although unfortunately they are also poisonous and can be very harmful.

Chrysanthemums

Chrysanthemums are beautiful bright flowers. A Chinese superstition says that if you drink chrysanthemum wine on the ninth day of the ninth month, you will have peace, good health, and old age. In Greece, chrysanthemums are believed to protect against evil spirits.

Xiaojun mushroom

Mirrors

Many years ago, people thought that witches used mirrors to practice "scrying"—a type of divination that gave the user a glimpse of the future through a reflective surface. Aztec priests used obsidian (polished volcanic glass) mirrors to try to conjure up visions, while the magician John Dee was said to use a mirror and crystal ball to talk with angels.

WITCH'S TOOLKIT

What might you find in a witch's toolkit? From cauldrons to magic wands, people have long believed that witches used special instruments to help weave their magic. Many of these tools were common household items that had been given extraordinary powers. How many do you recognize?

Cauldron

These large magical pots play an important role in Celtic myth. The Welsh enchantress Ceridwen used a cauldron to brew powerful potions, and in some folktales there is a cauldron that can bring the dead back to life. When the printing press was invented in the 15th century, a book was published that showed an illustration of witches stirring a cauldron to summon a storm. This cemented ideas about what witches looked like and how they behaved.

Wand

The magic wand is one of the most famous symbols of witchcraft. A wand is a long, thin rod, most commonly made from wood. In the ancient Greek poem, the *Odyssey*, the enchantress Circe uses a wand to transform men into pigs. In Italian fairy tales from the late Middle Ages, wands are the tools of powerful fairies. Today, stage magicians still use magic wands when performing their tricks.

Grimoire

This book of magic can be used to cast spells or perform rituals. The oldest grimoires come from ancient Mesopotamia, but they can be found throughout history and around the globe. Handwritten grimoires were very valuable, because they were thought to have magical powers. The Catholic Church disapproved of such books, and many were destroyed.

Broomstick

The image of a witch riding a broomstick through the night sky is one you might recognize. The first known picture of a witch riding a broomstick was printed in the 15th century. Today, followers of Wicca may use broomsticks in spells as a way to cleanse a space of negative energy.

Chalice

This ornate cup or goblet is a powerful tool in the modern religion of Wicca. In ancient cultures, it was thought a chalice could be used for divination. It is also an important symbol in many religions, including Christianity, where beautifully decorated chalices are used to celebrate Mass.

67

Tasseomancy

Telling the future using the patterns found in tea leaves or coffee grounds after the beverage has been drunk is called tasseomancy, or tasseography. Loose leaf tea is most popular, because it leaves swirling shapes at the bottom of a cup that can be interpreted to predict the drinker's future. It isn't known where tasseomancy first came from, but it is still practiced today.

Oneiromancy

Have you ever had a dream come true? Oneiromancy is the belief that we can study dreams to predict the future. This ancient art dates back to at least 3100 BCE, and can be found across most cultures. People believed that dreams were sent by the gods as prophecies or warnings. In the modern world, dreams are sometimes used to try and interpret unconscious activities of the brain.

DIVINATION

Divination is the art of predicting the future, often through supernatural means. Humans have always been curious about their destinies, and divination has been practiced across different cultures for thousands of years. Divination comes in many different forms, some of which are still popular today!

Palmistry

Palmistry uses the natural lines running across people's palms to predict their fortunes. It is practiced all around the world in many different cultures. During the Renaissance in Europe, it was considered a "forbidden art," and was banned by the Catholic Church. Witch hunters often looked for spots on the palm, interpreting them as signs of a pact with the Devil.

Rune casting
Runes are an ancient alphabet. Legend says that they were discovered by the Norse god Odin. Rune casting involves carving runes into sticks, stones, or bones and throwing them onto a smooth surface. Readers can divine the future from the way the runes fall.

Folklore and superstitions
In Celtic folklore, Halloween was thought to be a good time to practice divination. Young lovers might carry out a "nut burning" ritual, throwing hazelnuts into a fire and chanting a charm to see if their relationship would last.

"If you hate me, spit and fly. If you love me, burn away."

If the nuts jump from the heat, an unhappy future is foretold. If they burn quietly, the couple are believed to be a good match.

Astrology
Astrology is the art of studying the heavens—the stars, the sun, the moon, and the planets—and using their movements to predict the future. The first known organized system of astrology came from ancient Mesopotamia. There, people created the first zodiac wheel, which we still use to tell horoscopes today. Astrology soon traveled to India, Europe, and beyond, and has remained popular ever since.

Augury
Augury is a form of divination from ancient Greece and Rome. Augurs are people who interpret omens and signs from the gods by observing the behavior of birds. In Roman mythology, the brothers Romulus and Remus used augury to decide where to build a new city. Remus saw six vultures in his preferred location, but Romulus spied twelve in his, and went on to found the city of Rome!

I Ching
The *I Ching* is an ancient Chinese text used for divination. The book contains 64 hexagrams, which are piles of six lines, either broken or solid. Each hexagram represents something different, and users can create and compare their own hexagrams to those in the *I Ching* for spiritual guidance.

MODES of TRANSPORTATION

When you think of witches, you might also think of broomsticks. But did you know that witches have been thought to use many different types of transportation? From using flying ointment to enchanted sieves, witches traveled in some very unusual ways!

Broomstick

Humble broomsticks are now an iconic symbol of witchcraft, but why? Brooms were a common household tool, used for sweeping fireplaces and cleaning floors. Witchcraft was seen to be a household craft, so people imagined that witches might use everyday items for magical purposes. They also thought witches could fly using stalks of corn, blades of grass, or bundles of wheat! Witches that shape-shifted into animals were sometimes thought to ride on broomsticks too.

Flying ointment

Some people believed that witches made special ointments that gave them the power of flight. The ointments might be rubbed onto the skin or onto a mode of transportation, such as a broom or staff. Some recipes for flying ointments contain plants that cause visions.

Flying carpet

Amazing carpets with the power of flight appear in many stories of magic and adventure. In Russian fairy tales, the witch Baba Yaga helps Ivan the Fool by giving him a magical flying carpet. In *One Thousand and One Nights*, a collection of West Asian folk tales, Prince Husain buys a magic carpet from India. It was also said that King Solomon had a green silk carpet that could sail through the air.

Mortar and pestle

This kitchen tool is made up of a bowl and a club, and is used for crushing and grinding ingredients. It has been used for cooking and preparing medicines for thousands of years, which might be why it has been linked with magic. The Slavic witch, Baba Yaga, was believed to fly through the air in a bowl-shaped mortar, using the club-shaped pestle to steer. In other cultures, witches have been said to sail across water in sieves, egg shells, and sea shells.

Riding on animals

In some early modern European art, witches are shown riding on some unusual animals, from galloping on wolves to riding goats backward! Wolves were considered fearsome creatures that could only be tamed by dark magic, and goats, with their cloven hooves, were said to resemble Satan.

CELTIC MAGIC

The Celts were a group of different tribes who lived across Europe during the Iron Age. They were linked by language, and lived at a time when people believed in the power of nature. To them, Earth was sacred, with its own rhythms and energies.

Ceridwen
Welsh enchantress, and goddess of knowledge and rebirth

Ceridwen is a magical figure from Welsh mythology who lived by Bala Lake in North Wales. An enchantress of great power, she was the guardian of a magical cauldron and was associated with poetry and wisdom. Ceridwen had the ability to shape-shift into different animals, and could brew powerful potions. Modern Celtic pagans worship her as a goddess of knowledge, inspiration, and rebirth.

Brigid
Irish goddess of poetry and healing

Brigid is a Celtic goddess from pre-Christian Ireland. She is linked to poetry, wisdom, healing, protection, and blacksmiths. Her gifts made her a special goddess to those who loved art and literature. Brigid later became a saint in Christianity—St. Brigid, who is the "mother saint" of Ireland.

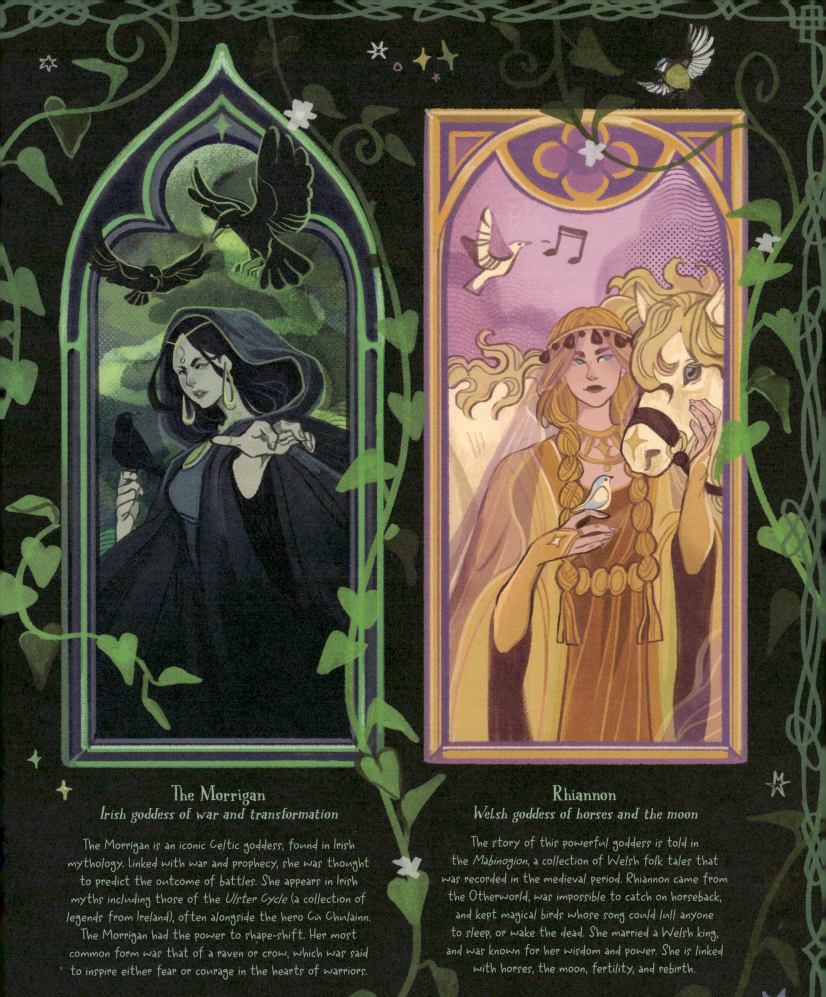

The Morrigan
Irish goddess of war and transformation

The Morrigan is an iconic Celtic goddess, found in Irish mythology. Linked with war and prophecy, she was thought to predict the outcome of battles. She appears in Irish myths including those of the *Ulster Cycle* (a collection of legends from Ireland), often alongside the hero Cú Chulainn. The Morrigan had the power to shape-shift. Her most common form was that of a raven or crow, which was said to inspire either fear or courage in the hearts of warriors.

Rhiannon
Welsh goddess of horses and the moon

The story of this powerful goddess is told in the *Mabinogion*, a collection of Welsh folk tales that was recorded in the medieval period. Rhiannon came from the Otherworld, was impossible to catch on horseback, and kept magical birds whose song could lull anyone to sleep, or wake the dead. She married a Welsh king, and was known for her wisdom and power. She is linked with horses, the moon, fertility, and rebirth.

73

ALICE KYTELER

Alice Kyteler lived in medieval Kilkenny, Ireland. In 1324, she became the first recorded person condemned for witchcraft in Ireland. After becoming a successful businesswoman, Alice was accused of sorcery and murder, and only narrowly escaped death.

In 13th-century Ireland, women were expected to marry and have children, rather than have careers of their own. Alice Kyteler was born into a wealthy family, and her first husband was a rich moneylender named William Outlaw. After Outlaw died, Alice and her son took over his business. She married three more times to rich men, and when each of them died, she and her son inherited their wealth.

By the time Alice married her fourth husband, Sir John le Poer, she was a successful businesswoman and had become very rich. Her stepchildren resented her—they felt that the money she had inherited should have been theirs and were suspicious that she had been married so many times. When John le Poer fell ill, they began to spread rumors that she was a poisoner.

ACCUSATIONS OF WITCHCRAFT

In 1324, Alice's stepchildren accused her and several members of her household of witchcraft, and asked the Bishop of Ossory to arrest her. Alice was accused of using flying ointment, talking with demons, sacrificing animals, using witchcraft to murder her husbands, and poisoning John le Poer.

The bishop demanded Alice's arrest, but Alice had powerful friends and the request was refused—instead, the Bishop was arrested! Once released, he ordered Alice to appear before him, but instead, she ran away to England.

A year later, Alice returned. Upset that the Bishop of Ossory had excommunicated her (banned her from the Catholic Church), she asked the Archbishop of Dublin to condemn him. But the bishop would not be defeated a second time: Alice and her friends were arrested and imprisoned in the dungeons of Kilkenny Castle. The punishment for their crimes was to be dragged through the streets, then burned at the stake.

ALICE'S ESCAPE

Faced with death, Alice looked to her friends for help. It is thought that Roger Outlaw, the brother of her first husband and Chancellor of Ireland, may have helped her escape. She fled to England once more and was never heard from again. Other members of Alice's household were not so lucky—her maid, Petronilla, was found guilty of heresy and executed.

Alice was an extraordinary woman, but her wealth and success made her many enemies. She is interesting because she was unlike many other people accused of witchcraft—in the centuries that followed, most of these were not rich or powerful. However, like Alice, many of them were women who did not fit society's expectations of their gender.

SHE WAS ACCUSED OF WITCHCRAFT AND POISONING.

Shamans usually communicate with spirits by entering a trance, which may involve chanting, drumming, or eating special plants.

Rootworkers use herbs, plants, and roots to treat both physical and spiritual problems.

Shamans

Found in regions of Siberia, Northern Europe, and Central Asia, shamans are spiritual leaders. They provide a link between their communities and the spirit world, offering guidance and wisdom. Sometimes, "shamanism" is used to refer to the spiritual practices of other Indigenous cultures. However, most cultures have their own name for such people, and follow different beliefs and traditions.

Hoodoo practitioners

Hoodoo is a set of spiritual traditions and beliefs, created by enslaved people in the southern United States. It combines different African spiritualities and Indigenous knowledge of plants and herbs. Practitioners of Hoodoo are sometimes called root doctors or rootworkers. They might treat illnesses and injuries using plants, or by performing rituals and spells.

MAGICAL HEALERS and CUNNING FOLK

Throughout history, most cultures have considered witches to be evil, but magic has not always been seen as bad. From medieval Europe to modern North America, many communities have relied on magical people who used their knowledge and powers for good. These people might be skilled in healing, or in contacting the spirit world, and often played a role in fighting harmful sorcery.

76

Mudang

Musok is a Korean folk religion, with many different deities, and is an important part of Korean culture. Musok's ritual spiritualists are called mudang, and they are usually women. Mudang can communicate with the spirit world and have the gift of divination.

Mudang perform rituals known as gut, which may involve singing, dancing, and leaving food and drink out for the gods.

Mother Shipton was an English herbalist and prophetess, who became well known for foretelling events such as the Great Fire of London and the defeat of the Spanish Armada.

Cunning folk

Practitioners of "low" or popular magic, cunning folk were usually well-known members of their community. They could be found across Europe, from the Middle Ages to the 20th century. Using charms or spells, they would help people with things like curing illnesses, attracting luck, or warding off evil magic. They might also talk with spirits or fairies, who they saw as "magical helpers."

The alchemist Jābir ibn Hayyān was obsessed with finding a potion that would give eternal life.

Alchemists

Alchemy is a mixture of magic and science. It was practiced by alchemists across many centuries and continents, from ancient Egypt to India and the Islamic world. They studied fantastic ideas, such as creating a "Philosopher's Stone" that could transform metals into gold or silver, and discovering a potion that could make the drinker immortal.

11

VODOU

This religion has roots in West Africa. In the 18th century, enslaved African people during the slave trade brought their beliefs to the Americas and combined them with Catholicism to form Vodou. It is now mainly practiced in Haiti and Louisiana. Followers of Vodou believe in one creator god called Bondye, as well as spirits called *lwa*. The religion has been linked to harmful witchcraft and magic, but this is a wrong idea formed by colonizers.

HISTORY

When enslaved Africans arrived in Haiti in the Caribbean, they were forced to obey France's "Code Noir," which banned all religions other than Catholicism. Traditional African religious practices were feared and thought to be using harmful magic, and people who practiced them would be punished. In spite of this, many enslaved Africans continued their spiritual practices in secret, fusing them with the traditions of Catholicism.

THE LWA

The *lwa* are the spirits of Vodou. They are created by Bondye, and their purpose is to guide the living. There are more than 1,000 *lwa*, each with their own personality and talents, and some are linked with specific Catholic saints. The *lwa* are worshipped with love and respect, and have the power to communicate with humans through dreams, divination, or possession.

A well-known Lwa, Papa Legba is guardian of the crossroads.

RITUALS AND PRACTICES

Vodou ceremonies are loud, joyful, and include everyone. They aim to summon spirits, and are led by an *oungan* (male priest) or *mambo* (female priestess), with drumming, singing, dancing, tracing *vévé* (spiritual drawings), and making offerings. During the ceremonies, the *lwa* are invited to join the living. Sometimes they might choose to "possess" a worshipper, so they can communicate with the congregation.

The vévé of Papa Legba

VODOU IS A SPIRITUAL RELIGION THAT GREW FROM PEOPLE WORKING TOGETHER AND STANDING UP FOR FREEDOM.

MISCONCEPTIONS

The French colonizers in Haiti feared Vodou, and saw it as a threat to their rule. The media has also shown Vodou in a bad light, linking it with witchcraft and sorcery, which is not true. It is a deeply spiritual religion, born out of standing up for freedom, but it is also a way of remembering the past, connecting with ancestors, and uniting with others.

CELEBRATIONS

Celebrations for important *lwa* usually take place on Saints' Days. Other feasts and festivals take place throughout the year. All Souls' Day is celebrated as *Fèt Gede*. It is a way to pay respects to people who have died and is one of the most important festivals of the year. People dress up, dance through the streets, and make offerings to the dead.

Chapter Four

A WORLD of NEW IDEAS

From the end of the medieval period, about 1500 CE, people began to travel farther than they ever had before. This meant that ideas and beliefs about witchcraft and magic began to travel quickly and widely as well. Ideas about witches spread in local communities, while the movement of people around the world due to the slave trade meant that some spiritual ideas began to blend with others, creating brand-new magical beliefs. This was a time of great change, and the world would never be the same.

The RISE of WITCH HUNTS

The early modern period (1450-1780) in Europe was a time of disruption. Religious wars, famine, and disease meant there was a lot of hardship in daily life. People began to fear that these problems meant the Devil's power was growing, and that his servants were practicing harmful magic. These fears led to many people being wrongly accused of and punished for witchcraft.

RELIGIOUS TENSIONS

In the 1500s, the teachings of a German priest, Martin Luther, started the Reformation—an event that split the Christian Church into Catholics, who followed the Pope, and Protestants, who did not. Each side thought their beliefs were right, and bitter wars were fought between them. Both groups began to fear the Devil's growing power, and thought that removing heretics (people whose beliefs were against their religion) and those who practiced harmful magic would help people see that theirs was the true faith.

SOCIAL STRUGGLES

This period was also a time of great change in society. A "Little Ice Age" hit Europe, causing crops to die and famine to spread. Then, to make matters worse, the Black Death swept through the continent between 1346 and 1351, killing up to half of the population. People feared that supernatural forces had brought the plague to their doors. After this destruction, there was unrest in most of Europe. In these religious and superstitious societies, it was easy to blame the events on witches and harmful magic.

WITCH HUNTING HANDBOOKS

During the 15th century, books and pamphlets attacking witchcraft began to be published, including the *Formicarius* and the *Errores Gazariorum*. The most famous of these, published in 1487, was the *Malleus Maleficarum*, meaning "The Hammer of Witches," by Heinrich Kramer. It taught people how to identify and punish witches, and grew very popular. During the Renaissance, scholars became interested in demons, and thought witches made pacts with them and the Devil. The *Malleus Maleficarum* and other publications spread these views to larger audiences.

The invention of the European printing press in 1436 meant books and pamphlets could be printed and distributed cheaply to a large number of people.

WOMEN AND THE WITCH HUNTS

In this period, women did not have many rights. The *Malleus Maleficarum* used untrue beliefs about women to suggest they were more likely to be witches. It said they were greedier and more foolish than men, so could be tricked or tempted into working with the Devil. It also claimed they liked to gossip, and would teach each other "evil arts." Women who did not fit in, such as the old, poor, or widowed, were more likely to be accused of witchcraft, because people saw their differences as something to be feared.

EUROPEAN WITCH TRIALS

Between the 15th and 18th centuries, witch hunts spread across Europe and around 30,000 people were executed. Most of those accused were women, and came from poor backgrounds. While Scotland, Scandinavia, and Western Germany were host to many mass trials, execution for witchcraft was rare in Spain, Italy, and other countries in Southern Europe.

1. Kilkenny, Ireland (1324)
Alice Kyteler, her son, and her household are accused of witchcraft and murder. Alice escapes, but her servant Petronilla is executed.

2. Valais, Switzerland (1428-1447)
In one of Europe's earliest witch trials, at least 367 men and women are accused of witchcraft and executed.

3. Val Camonica, Italy (1505-1510 and 1518-1521)
This region of Italy has long been suspected of paganism. Two waves of witch trials see hundreds of people executed for sorcery.

16. Doruchów, Poland (1775)
One of the last mass witch trials in Europe, the Doruchów witch trial saw up to 14 women executed. It may have led to a ban on witch burning in Poland. However, some historians question whether it really happened!

15. Salzburg, Austria (1675-1690)
One of the most famous witch trials takes place in Salzburg, Austria. Almost all of the accused are men. 139 people are executed for following "Wizard Jackl"—a man who is never captured. 39 of those killed are children, and most are beggars or homeless.

14. Torsåker, Sweden (1674-1675)
The largest witch trial in Sweden takes place in Torsåker, after Protestant leaders spread rumors of witchcraft and sorcery in their parishes. 71 people are executed in a single day.

13. Lukh, Russia (1656-1660)
One of the biggest witch trials in Russia takes place in the village of Lukh, near Moscow. 25 people are accused of casting spells to cause fits and illness, and five are executed. Most of the accused are men.

12. East Anglia, England (1645-1647)
Under the judgment of "Witchfinder General" Matthew Hopkins, and during the English Civil War, at least 1,000 people are accused and 100 people executed for witchcraft in East Anglia.

4. Navarre,
Spain (1525-1526)

After the Council of Navarre sends a special commissioner to investigate the people living in the North Pyrenees mountains, a number of witch trials take place.

5. Trier,
Germany (1581-1593)

Archbishop Johann von Schönenberg attempts to root out "witches" in the Catholic German town of Trier. Around 368 people are executed.

6. North Berwick,
Scotland (1590)

King James VI and his new wife nearly drown on their return from Denmark, and witchcraft is blamed. Nearly 70 people, including Scottish nobility, are accused.

7. Copenhagen,
Denmark (1590-1591)

The first major witch trial in Denmark takes place in Copenhagen. 17 people are executed in a trial linked to the North Berwick witch trial and the storms that put the royal fleet in danger.

8. Aix-en-Provence,
France (1611)

When a group of nuns fall victim to "demonic possession" in southern France, a priest called Father Louis Gaufridi is accused of enchanting them by making a pact with the Devil. He is found guilty and is executed. A similar case takes place 20 years later in Loudun, France.

9. Pendle, England (1612)

In the English county of Lancashire, a teenager called Alizon Device "curses" a local man. Her younger sister, Jennet, gives evidence at the trial and accuses her whole family of witchcraft. 12 people are executed.

11. Bamberg,
Germany (1626-1631)

One of the biggest witch trials in history takes place during the Thirty Years War—a religious conflict between Protestants and Catholics. About 1,000 people are executed for witchcraft.

10. Vardø, Norway (1621)

A freak storm drowns many of the men of Vardø, Northern Norway. Soon after, at trial, some of the accused confess that "witches" were responsible. Two more large witch trials in Vardø follow. Many of those held and executed are Sami people.

85

JOAN of ARC

Joan was born during the Hundred Years War—a medieval war between France and England—and was deeply religious. She believed that God had called upon her to save the French. Joan defied all expectations of women at the time, riding at the head of the French army, before being executed by her enemies.

Joan was born to a poor family in 1412 in Donrémy, France. As a girl, Joan would have been expected to marry and spend her life carrying out domestic work. However, when she turned 13, Joan began to hear voices—she believed they were the archangel Michael, Saint Margaret, and Saint Catherine. They told her God had chosen her for a special mission: she was to lead the French to victory in their war against England. She soon set off on her divine quest.

Joan the warrior
In 1428, Joan arrived in Vaucouleurs with a small party of followers. She wanted to meet Charles of Valois, the crown prince of France, to explain her mission. However, he was in Chinon, which was an 11 day march away, behind enemy territory. Unafraid, Joan cut off her long hair and disguised herself as a man to make the journey. When she reached Chinon, Joan asked Charles for an army to fight the English. He believed Joan's story and agreed. Joan dressed in armor and led the French into battle on horseback, forcing the English to retreat.

Joan accused as a witch
After Joan's victory, her reputation as a divine warrior spread. In 1430, she was captured by English allies and handed over to her enemies. She was put on trial by the English for witchcraft, heresy, and dressing as a man. Despite their friendship, Charles, who was now king, did not send anyone to help her and Joan was found guilty.

Joan's legacy
At the age of only 19, Joan was executed. As an accused witch, her punishment was to be burned at the stake. In 1920, Joan was made a saint. She is considered one of the Catholic Church's most loyal followers, one of history's greatest martyrs, and the patron saint of France. Pope Benedict XV claimed that her life was "a proof of the existence of God."

WITCH'S MARK

A "Devil's mark" or "witch's mark" was a place on a witch's body where people believed the Devil had touched them, and was seen as a symbol of the agreement they had made. It was also thought that it might be where a familiar would feed from! Often, people's natural freckles, moles, or birthmarks were wrongly identified as witch's marks.

DUCKING

Ducking, or swimming, a witch is one of the most famous methods of trial. Suspected witches would be dragged to a pond or river, and their hands and legs would be bound. They would then be dunked, or "ducked," beneath the water, using either a "ducking stool" or a rope around their waist. People believed that water was holy and would reject evil. Suspects who floated were therefore confirmed as "witches" and those who sank were considered innocent. Although the innocent would then be pulled from the water, it was too late for some victims of this watery judgment.

METHODS of TRYING A WITCH

If someone was accused of witchcraft, they might be made to stand trial. However, witchcraft was a secret crime that often took place under the cover of darkness with no witnesses. How could you prove that someone was a witch? In early modern Europe, people had many techniques they believed would prove that someone was guilty. Of course, most people were making up their stories about people being witches out of fear or spite.

LORD'S PRAYER

Some people believed that witches, as servants of the Devil (people who did evil), were unable to recite the words of the Bible. A common method of trying a witch was to ask them to say the Lord's Prayer, a famous Christian prayer, out loud. If they stumbled over words or made a mistake, it would confirm to those watching that the suspect was indeed a "witch." However, many of the accused would not have known how to read or write, and the pressure of the trial might have made them trip over their tongues!

TOUCH TEST

The touch test was one way to determine whether a suspect was really a witch. People often believed that if someone suffered a sudden illness, fit, or madness, it was the result of witchcraft. In these cases, a suspected witch would be made to lay their hand upon the suffering person. If the victim calmed or got better, it was seen as proof that their illness had come from that "witch." If there was no reaction, the accused was considered to be innocent.

WITCH CAKE

A witch cake was a special (and revolting) dessert used to identify a "witch" suspected of causing someone harm. Rye meal, ashes, and a sample of the victim's urine were all mixed together and baked into a "cake." The cake was fed to a pet, such as a cat or a dog, because animals were often believed to be witches' familiars. If the pet developed the same symptoms as the victim, it was seen as proof that the victim's illness was caused by witchcraft. It was also hoped that the pet would then reveal the name of the guilty witch!

PRICKING

Some people believed they could find a witch's "Devil's mark" by pricking them with a pin until they found a place on their body that didn't hurt—where the Devil was supposed to have left his mark. Matthew Hopkins, a famous witch hunter, is thought to have used a pricker with a point that collapsed, so he could make people think they had been pricked without hurting them, and therefore accuse them of being guilty of witchcraft.

Philipp Adolf von Ehrenberg

Between 1625 and 1631, some of Europe's largest witch trials took place in Würzburg, Germany. We don't know what sparked the mass trials, but accusations of witchcraft spiraled out of control and hundreds of men, women, and even children were executed. The trials were overseen by the Prince-Bishops of Würzburg, and the reign of Philipp Adolf von Ehrenberg saw 900 people executed, including his nephew!

WITCH HUNTERS

Some people prided themselves on their ability to recognize workers of bad magic—some of these "witch hunters" were even responsible for the trial and execution of hundreds of people. But why did they do it? Witch hunters were often well paid and, at a time when most people believed in the power of harmful magic, they may truly have thought they were keeping their communities safe.

"John Dickson" Christian Caldwell

Christian Caldwell was a Scottish woman who disguised herself as a man named "John Dickson." She did this so she could become a well-paid "witch pricker"—someone who identified "witches" by pricking them with pins. Christian's true identity was discovered after she wrongly accused an important court messenger. She was put on trial and banished to a plantation in Barbados in 1663.

Matthew Hopkins

Along with his colleague John Stearne, Matthew Hopkins was responsible for the trial and execution of around 300 people during the English Civil War (1642-1651). Hopkins declared himself the unofficial "Witchfinder General" and traveled around the east of England, looking for "witches." Villagers and townspeople paid him well, and he soon developed a terrifying reputation. Hopkins used brutal methods on the accused, including sleep deprivation and pricking.

Tenskwatawa

Tenskwatawa was a religious leader of the Native American Shawnee tribe. He wanted his people to keep their traditional values and ways of life, and was unhappy about the European colonists who had invaded their land. He did not want the Shawnee to interact with them, and treated those who disagreed with him badly. Tenskwatawa accused such people of witchcraft, and was responsible for the deaths of many Indigenous people.

Nicholas Rémy

Born in 1530, Nicholas Rémy was a French witch hunter. When he was a child, he witnessed several witchcraft trials, and this experience sparked a lifelong obsession. In 1583, he became a lawyer, responsible for a large region called the Duchy of Lorraine. During this time, he tried and executed as many suspected witches as possible. In his book, *Daemonolatreiae*, he claimed to be responsible for the death of more than 800 "witches."

Sebastien Michaelis

Sebastien Michaelis was a French priest, and during the 1580s, he was involved in a number of witch trials. He later developed an interest in demons, and considered himself a "demonologist." By 1611, he was a terrifying interrogator and was asked to investigate a nun thought to be possessed by a demon. A local priest, Father Louis Gaufridi, was accused of enchanting her, and Michaelis tortured him until he confessed. Gaufridi was found guilty and executed.

The SABBATH

A day of rest in religions such as Judaism and Christianity is known as a Sabbath. The Bible says "remember the Sabbath day, and keep it holy," meaning that, while the rest of the week was for work, the Sabbath was for rest and worshipping God. In early modern Europe, people believed witches held their own Sabbaths, when they would gather to cast spells and work dark magic.

Witches' Sabbaths were the opposite of religious days of rest. They were said to happen during the dead of night and, instead of praying, witches feasted on rich foods, danced around wildly, and worshipped the Devil. Sabbaths supposedly took place in wild, remote locations, such as deep in woods or on windy moors.

The Sabbath and Witch Hunts

At first, the Sabbath was mostly written about by scholars and priests, and was not part of popular beliefs about witchcraft. But after the printing press was invented, people could learn more about the world through printed words and images.

As a result, pictures of the Sabbath, along with stories from trials, made their way into people's imaginations. When people accused of witchcraft were questioned, they were often asked whether they had attended a Sabbath and whether anyone else had been there.

Hoping for a lighter punishment, the accused might claim they had seen other people from their town there, which caused the trials to grow in size.

PEOPLE STARTED TO IMAGINE STORIES OF THE SABBATH.

Night Battles
During the 16th and 17th centuries, there was a group of farm workers in Italy called the *benandanti* ("good walkers"). The *benandanti* claimed that while they were sleeping, they could travel outside their bodies. During the night, they would battle against evil witches to make sure the next season's crops would be good. In witch trials throughout Europe, a number of *benandanti* were accused of witchcraft themselves, when their night battles were confused with the witches' Sabbath.

Flying to the Sabbath
People believed that witches rubbed an ointment onto themselves or their broomsticks that allowed them to fly through the night to the Sabbath. Some of the recipes for this ointment have survived. Many of the ingredients were plants which, when rubbed into the skin, cause hallucinations.

Wiccan Sabbaths
The modern religion of Wicca celebrates "Sabbats" over the year, including the summer and winter solstices. They usually happen when the seasons change, and are a time for feasting, celebration, and reflection.

MEXICAN INQUISITION

CURANDERAS

Curanderas and *curanderos* are folk healers. Their methods of healing, known as *curanderismo*, included herbal medicine, midwifery, and communication with the spirit world. These practices, and the fact that many *curanderas* were women, meant the Inquisition accused many of them of witchcraft. Despite this, *curanderas* often escaped punishment, because their medical skills and knowledge made them an important part of their communities.

During the 16th century, European countries raced against one another to grab land and set up colonies in the "New World" of the Americas—despite the fact that there were already people living there. In 1521, a Spanish conquistador, Hernán Cortés, and his army defeated the mighty Aztec Empire and took control of much of what is now Mexico. Spanish Catholics saw the beliefs and rituals of Mexico's Indigenous peoples as dangerous, so they set up the Mexican Inquisition to convert them to Catholicism and stamp out their beliefs.

THE MEXICAN INQUISITION

The Inquisition accused many Mexicans of witchcraft and sorcery. Their "witchcraft," known as *brujería*, was actually a mixture of Indigenous beliefs, Spanish religion, and divination rituals from enslaved African people. Those found guilty were threatened with a terrible execution: burning alive at the stake.

A culture of fear and suspicion set in. Neighbors accused neighbors, and whole families turned on one another. Everyone was scared they would be taken by the Inquisition—unless they accused someone else first.

SOLEDAD'S STORY

Soledad was a skilled herbalist and *curandera* from the city of Córdoba, Mexico. When the Mayor of Córdoba, Don Martín de Ocaña, tried to win Soledad's affections, she gently rejected him. Don Martín became angry, and spread rumors that she was a "witch" and had drugged him with a love potion.

The townspeople loved Soledad, but were scared that the Mexican Inquisition would punish them if they did not support Don Martín's accusations. When questioned, they swore they had seen her flying over the city at night and that she had forced them to sell her love potions.

Soledad was found guilty of witchcraft and sentenced to death. As she wondered from her prison cell how she might escape her fate, she had an idea…

She asked a prison guard to bring her a piece of charcoal so she could amuse herself by drawing on the wall. The guard watched in amazement as Soledad sketched, in great detail, a ship sailing on the ocean.

"What do you think?" she asked. "Is anything missing?"

The guard shrugged. "I don't think so, it looks perfect to me. But perhaps the ship needs a captain?"

Soledad laughed. "You're right!" she said, and before the guard could blink, she jumped aboard the ship and sailed off through the walls of the prison.

People still believe Soledad haunts Córdoba. Some say they have seen her flying through the night, while others report strange lights and chanting from the house where she used to live. A ghostly ship has even been said to emerge from the prison walls with Soledad on board.

COLONIALISM AND WITCHCRAFT

Colonialism is when one country takes over a place and the people living there by force. Between the 15th and 20th centuries, European settlers colonized many areas around the globe. But these areas were not empty. The people who lived there, known as Indigenous people, were treated badly by colonizers. Indigenous traditions were not respected or understood by Europeans. In some colonized places, beliefs were mistaken for witchcraft. Colonizers tried to impose their own, mostly Christian, beliefs onto Indigenous people instead.

MISUNDERSTANDING HEALERS

When the Portuguese entered the Kingdom of Kongo in Central Africa in 1483, they did not understand many of the local customs or beliefs. The *nganga*—divine healers who cured disease and protected people from evil spirits—were accused of being sorcerers and Devil-worshippers. In North America, Indigenous spiritual leaders were respected as knowledgeable healers and worked to protect their communities from supernatural harm, but European colonizers thought they were practicing harmful magic.

Indigenous healers in Canada

KEEPING POWER

In Jamaica, British colonizers used the term *Obeah* to describe the religious, magical, and healing traditions practiced by enslaved Africans. Worried *Obeah* was being used to fight against them, colonizers declared it illegal in 1760. Despite this, the practice has survived in Jamaica. *Obeah* men and women have special gifts which they use to help people, from curing illnesses to removing spells. Some people think that *Obeah* should be made legal again, and are campaigning to have the law removed.

An *Obeah* figure stolen from a man in Jamaica

DISRESPECTING RITUALS

European colonizers often failed to understand the rituals of other cultures. When they arrived in new places, they often had fixed views about the people who lived there, which were wrong. For example, Inuit peoples of the Arctic and Northern Europe believed in many gods. Their healers, called *angakkuq*, carried out special rites to help their hunters catch enough food for winter. But when European colonizers first came into contact with the Inuits in around 1500 CE, they saw these practices as witchcraft instead of respecting their beliefs.

Colonizers arriving in Northern Europe

LAND AND RELIGION

Colonizers often wanted to take over lands because they contained valuable resources, such as gold or sugar. The Yanomami are a group of Indigenous people living in the Amazon rainforest, who believe each part of nature has a spirit. In the 1950s, the Yanomami's land was invaded by loggers and people mining for gold. To this day, the Yanomami are threatened for their resource-rich land.

Colonizers tried to force Indigenous peoples to abandon their beliefs, and to accept the colonizers' laws and religion, so they could be controlled easily. These views led to inequalities in society that are still felt by Indigenous people around the world today.

A Yanomami shaman from Brazil

97

MAGICAL OBJECTS

Magical objects feature in many myths and legends around the world. From granting wishes to bestowing supernatural powers, these items often help their owners escape danger or complete quests. Some are found in folk or fairy tales, while others have religious or spiritual significance. Can you think of any magical objects?

Cap of Invisibility
In ancient Greek mythology, the Cap of Invisibility was a helmet that could turn the wearer invisible. It was said to have been given to Hades by Zeus, king of the gods, during a war. It was also used by the war goddess Athena, the messenger god Hermes, and the hero Perseus.

Magic hammer
In Japanese legend, the magic hammer, known as *uchide no kozuchi*, is a wooden tool that features in many popular stories. The hammer is said to be able to tap out anything that is wished for, from plentiful riches to happiness and good fortune. It is often found in the hand of Daikoku-ten, a deity of wealth and prosperity.

Censer
A censer is a special object made for burning incense, and is linked to religious or spiritual practices. In China and West Asia, censers have been found in the shape of lions, birds, cows, and other animals. Mayans painted their censers with colorful images and used them when communicating with the gods.

Cintamani stone
Found in both Hindu and Buddhist traditions, the Cintamani stone is a magical jewel with the power to grant wishes. In Hinduism, it is often depicted being held by the god Vishnu and is a beautiful red ruby. Some Buddhists believe it takes the form of a glistening pearl, and is held by the Buddha himself.

Seven-League boots
The seven-league boots are a magical pair of boots that allow the wearer to take strides seven leagues long when they are walking. The length of a league is disputed, but it could have been about 2.4 miles (3.9 km)! The boots appear in several different European folk and fairy tales, most famously in the stories of the French writer Charles Perrault.

PENDLE WITCH TRIALS

Imagine being nine years old and helping to imprison your own family for witchcraft. That's what happened to Jennet Device in Lancashire, England, in one of the most famous witch trials of the 17th century. James I was king, and he was so terrified of witches that he wrote a book about them called *Daemonologie*. People began to suspect witches everywhere!

Pendle, a small district in Lancashire, England, was hardly more than a scattering of villages in the 17th century, huddled in the shadow of Pendle Hill. Life for many people was very hard. Nine-year-old Jennet Device lived with her mother Elizabeth, her sister Alizon, her brother James, and her grandmother Demdike. The family were extremely poor, and lived in a house called Malkin Tower. Demdike was known to be a "cunning woman"—someone who used magic.

The Devices did not like their neighbors, Anne Whittle (known as Chattox) and her daughter Anne Redferne. Chattox's family had stolen from the Device family years before, and they had not been forgiven.

The Curse

One day, Alizon Device was out begging and a peddler passed by, carrying items for sale. She asked him for one of the silver pins he carried in his bag, but he refused. Angry, Alizon cursed him. As she did, the peddler's face turned pale and he slumped to one side and fell to the ground. Terrified, Alizon ran home to confess what she had done.

The next day, she went to see the peddler. Alizon cried and begged for his forgiveness, but it was too late. The crime was reported to the local magistrate, Roger Nowell.

Nowell questioned Alizon and she admitted cursing the peddler. However, she also accused Chattox and Anne Redferne of bewitching and murdering four people. When they were brought in, they retaliated by accusing Granny Demdike of being a "witch!" Nowell arrested Alizon and Demdike, as well as their neighbors.

The Good Friday Gathering

Alizon's mother Elizabeth held a party at their home in Malkin Tower for people who wanted to help Alizon and Demdike. It was Good Friday, a holy day before Easter. A local policeman heard about the gathering and arrested everyone there, including Alizon's mother and her brother. They were all accused of witchcraft.

The Trial

The trial was very shocking. Roger Nowell made Alizon's young sister Jennet give evidence in court against her own family. Children were not usually allowed to do this, so this was a special case. Nowell also wanted to punish Catholics, and the trial claimed that the women had been practicing Catholic prayers.

When Jennet entered the room, her mother Elizabeth screamed in horror. Jennet showed no emotion and asked that Elizabeth be removed from the room. She then calmly told the court that her mother was a "witch." The trial lasted two days. Of the people accused, twelve were found guilty of witchcraft and hanged.

This included all of Jennet's family.

The Aftermath

Pendle soon became one of the most famous witch trials in England. We don't know how Jennet felt about the death of her family, or about having played a role in it. But 20 years later, her fortunes changed.

She herself was accused of witchcraft by ten-year-old Edmund Robinson. One night in 1633, Edmund went out and did not come home until dark. His clothes were torn and his face was muddy. Worried, his parents asked what had happened. Edmund recited a story of being kidnapped by "witches" who could turn into animals. He claimed that he had seen them feasting in a barn, but had escaped and run away. One of the women he said was there was Jennet Device.

Edmund became a local celebrity, reciting his story in nearby villages. Many people were arrested because of his accusations. Before long, however, Edmund admitted that he was lying. He had made it all up after hearing about the Pendle trials of 1612.

The last we know of Jennet Device is that she was still imprisoned in the Lancaster jail in 1636, probably because she was too poor to pay for her release.

SALEM WITCH TRIALS

In 1692, the small village of Salem in Massachusetts was rocked by the most infamous witch trials of the Americas. Over the next year, more than 150 people would be accused of witchcraft, resulting in 19 executions. By May 1693, it was all over, but for many this was too late. What caused such hysteria? And who were the "witches" at the heart of the story?

Salem was an area on the coast of Massachusetts, and in the 17th century, it was split into two parts. Salem Town was based around the port, and was a thriving community with wealthy citizens. Salem Village was poorer, and depended heavily on farming. This divide created tension between families on the two sides of Salem.

In 1689, Reverend Samuel Parris became the minister for Salem Village. He was fiercely religious and began to preach warnings about the Devil's presence in the world.

THE FIRST ACCUSERS

Betty Parris
(9 years old)

Abigail Williams
(11 years old)

Ann Putnam Jr.
(12 years old)

Elizabeth Hubbard
(17 years old)

STRANGE BEGINNINGS

In January 1692, Samuel Parris's daughter Betty and her cousin Abigail began to have strange outbursts where their bodies jerked violently and they fell into fits of screaming. A local doctor declared they were bewitched and, before long, other young girls in the community became sick with the same symptoms.

The girls soon accused three women on the edges of society of bewitching them: the elderly Sarah Osborne; Sarah Good, an impoverished woman; and Tituba, a woman who was enslaved by the Parris family. After she was beaten and forced to confess, Tituba described a pact she had made with the Devil, and accused others in the community of acting alongside her.

THE FIRST ACCUSED

Sarah Osborne
A farm owner

Sarah Good
An impoverished pregnant woman

Tituba
A woman enslaved by the Parris family

The trials

Hysteria spread throughout Salem and beyond, as more and more "witches" were accused—even the four-year-old daughter of Sarah Good was suspected of dark magic! In May 1692, an official court was set up to decide their fate. Much of the evidence against the accused was "spectral"— wild stories about dreams and visions that could not be proven. An author called Cotton Mather warned that this should not be enough to find someone guilty, but the judges ignored him and took the tales of "spectral" harm very seriously. Over the next three months, 19 people were hanged, while several others died in jail.

A somber end

In October 1692, Cotton's father, Increase Mather, also condemned the use of "spectral evidence." He said, "It were better that ten suspected witches should escape than that one innocent person should be condemned." The tide was turning. By the time the trials began again in early 1693, the hysteria that had gripped Salem was over. Those convicted or held in jail were pardoned. The leading judge, Samuel Sewall, apologized for his role in the trials soon after.

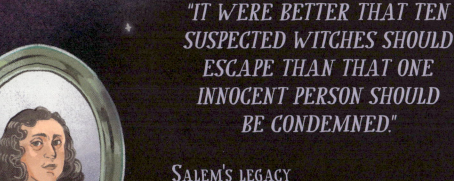

↑ Increase Mather

"IT WERE BETTER THAT TEN SUSPECTED WITCHES SHOULD ESCAPE THAN THAT ONE INNOCENT PERSON SHOULD BE CONDEMNED."

Salem's legacy

The Salem witch trials have been studied, and have inspired many works of art and literature, including Arthur Miller's play *The Crucible*. Nobody knows what caused the mysterious fits in the young girls of Salem.

Salem's legacy is more than just fear and shame: it also changed the criminal justice system in the US. Now, anyone accused of a crime has a right to legal representation, and is presumed innocent rather than guilty.

WHAT CAUSED the WITCH HUNTS?

Why did a wave of witch hunts spread across early modern Europe in the 15th to 18th centuries? This question has puzzled historians for a long time. The size of the trials varied from region to region, and there is no single obvious cause. It is likely that the trials were the result of many different factors, which included social tensions, religious conflict, unsettled weather, and changes to the legal system.

CLIMATE CHANGE

During the early modern period, Europe went through a time of climate change known as the "Little Ice Age." Cooler temperatures led to strange weather events and crops dying, causing famine and misery. Looking for someone to blame for their misfortune, people accused witches of raising storms and bringing sickness upon livestock.

SOCIAL ISSUES

In times of hardship, tensions could build in towns and villages, and accusations of witchcraft often happened after arguments between neighbors. Poor or homeless people might be called witches too. People felt guilty for not showing them enough Christian charity—it was easier to accuse those in need than to admit you were not giving them enough.

RELIGIOUS CONFLICT

By the 14th century, magic was seen as heresy. The trials for heretics in this time were similar to the witch trials that followed. After the 16th-century Protestant Reformation, Catholics and Protestants both wanted to convince people that theirs was the right faith. They each thought that fighting witches and demons would prove God preferred them.

TECHNOLOGICAL PROGRESS

The invention of the printing press meant that information and images could be created and shared more easily. Books such as the *Malleus Maleficarum* and prints of art showing witches made people afraid that witches were all around them. During the witch hunts, people often published pamphlets with details of the trials and the confessions of the accused. The details would then be used in later trials.

LEGAL CHANGES

In early times, if you accused someone of a crime and they were found innocent, this could result in punishment for you. However, after the 13th century, this changed—accusing someone no longer held any danger, so people were more likely to point their fingers at others. Witchcraft was also seen as a "secret crime," so reliable eye witnesses were not needed to find someone guilty.

WAS WITCH HUNTING "WOMEN HUNTING"?

Witch hunting was not women hunting, yet more than 70 percent of people accused of witchcraft were women. They were more likely to be suspected of witchcraft because people believed untrue things about their characters, they didn't fit in, or they lacked power in a society that was controlled by men. Old, poor, and widowed women were particularly at risk.

NORTH AMERICA and MAGIC

An Indigenous person from the Chesapeake region of the US

North America is a large continent that spans 23 countries, including Canada and the US. The first humans came to North America around 30,000 years ago. In the US, these Indigenous people are known as Native Americans, while in Canada they are commonly referred to as First Nations. The Arctic Circle is home to Inuit peoples. After the 15th century, Europeans began to colonize North America, bringing with them ideas about magic and witchcraft that were different from those held by the Indigenous peoples.

INDIGENOUS CULTURES

Across North America, there are many different Indigenous cultures. When Europeans arrived, there were probably more than 200 separate nations, each with their own beliefs and traditions. Most nations felt a deep connection to nature, and believed that each creature and plant had their own spirit. Indigenous spiritual leaders were called "medicine men" by colonizers, even though this was not what most of them called themselves. The role of these men and women was to heal and protect their communities from spiritual harm.

A family from the Cherokee Nation in the US

COLONIZERS AND WITCHCRAFT

The word "witchcraft" arrived with European colonizers, but many cultures had stories about people who used their power over the spirit world for evil. These people were shunned and punished. Europeans did not understand the difference between this magic and that of "medicine men," so they labeled Indigenous rituals as harmful magic. Over the next centuries, Indigenous people were driven from their land and punished for practicing their cultural traditions.

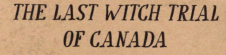

CANADIAN LEGENDS

After 1534, French colonizers settled in eastern Canada, and named it New France. There was less enthusiasm for witch hunting there, but they had many tales of mysterious flying canoes. These came from mixing Indigenous legends with a French folk tale in which a hunter was sentenced to be chased through the sky forever after missing Sunday Mass!

THE LAST WITCH TRIAL OF CANADA

Maggie Pollock was born in 1879 in Huron County, Canada, and worked as a housekeeper on her brother's farm. While she was still a young girl, Maggie realized she was unusual: she seemed to have a gift for seeing and hearing things that other people could not.

In about 1900, Maggie had two visions—she claimed to have seen the first modern airplanes and cars, years before they were even invented. She was able to use her gifts to find lost items, and her neighbors often came to her for help when their things had been misplaced or stolen. Some thought she was a "witch," but Maggie always insisted that her powers came from God.

In 1919, Maggie was brought to Huron County Jail, accused of "telling fortunes." This was illegal in Canada at the time, under a law that stated that anyone "pretending" to practice witchcraft or the occult was guilty of fraud. Although Maggie was convicted, many of her neighbors were upset with the way she had been treated. She received letters from far and wide and was even contacted by policemen to help them search for missing people and solve murder cases. By the time she died in 1934, she was a well-respected member of her community. She was the last Canadian woman to be charged with witchcraft.

AFRICAN WITCHCRAFT

From deserts in the north to grasslands in the south, Africa is a richly diverse continent. It is home to many different peoples, each with their own traditions, histories, and religious rituals. In many African cultures, magic plays a significant role.

THE MAKA PEOPLE

The Maka live in the rainforest region of southeast Cameroon. For them, witchcraft, known as *djambe* or *sorcellerie*, covers many things, from harmful magic to healing. There is a strong link between witchcraft and family, and they believe that anyone can have *djambe* inside them. In powerful witches, *djambe* is said to leave their body at night and commit evil deeds.

THE AZANDE PEOPLE

The Azande people live in South Sudan, the Democratic Republic of the Congo, and the Central African Republic. The Azande believe in the power of witchcraft, and blame it for a range of misfortunes, big or small. They think witches are born that way, and that their power grows as they get older. For the Azande, witchcraft is different from sorcery: witchcraft happens from willpower and intent alone, while sorcery is achieved through charms and spells.

SANGOMAS

These highly respected healers in Zulu culture are from Southern Africa. Sangomas are thought to protect people against witchcraft through divination. They practice *Ngoma*, which involves calling on ancestral spirits for guidance. Summoning the ancestors may involve drumming, dancing, and singing. Through the Sangomas, the spirits provide advice on protection and healing.

JUJU

A system of West African magical beliefs, Juju usually refers to objects that have been deliberately charged with magic. They can be used for good or bad, depending on whether they have come into contact with positive or negative energies. Negative Juju might cause illness and misfortune, while protective Juju amulets are worn to ward away evil or help with healing.

Naguals

Naguals or *nahuales* can be found in many Mesoamerican spiritual traditions. They are humans who have the ability to shape-shift into animals. These animals are known as their *tonal* and are seen as their spiritual counterparts. They can use their powers for good or bad, depending on their personality.

Leyaks

These shape-shifters come from Balinese folklore. During the day, *Leyaks* appear as human, but at night, they transform into disembodied heads and fly through the air, seeking victims. They are ruled over by a witch queen named Rangda, who plays an important role in rituals and festivals.

WHAT IS A SHAPE-SHIFTER?

Shape-shifters are creatures who can change their form. From the earliest history to the present day, many cultures around the globe have believed in shape-shifters. Some people associate witchcraft and harmful magic with the ability to shape-shift.

SHAPE-SHIFTERS and FAMILIARS

Throughout history, some cultures have believed witches were able to transform themselves into certain creatures. Others have suspected that witches formed bonds with "familiar spirits" who would do their bidding. In parts of Northern Europe, people thought that witches would turn into hares, using this disguise to steal milk from their neighbors' cows!

Louhi

This powerful queen of Finnish mythology rules over the land of Pohjola, and has the ability to change her shape and weave powerful spells. Louhi is the enemy of the hero Väinämöinen and his friends in an epic poem called the *Kalevala*.

Toads
The humble toad is a popular witch's familiar, and some witchcraft confessions describe feeding a toad blood or milk in return for a special substance from its body. This could then be used in ointments and magical rituals.

Mice
Common household nuisances, mice can regularly be seen stealing food and slipping in and out of rooms. Their ability to squeeze through the tightest of spaces so they can come and go as they please make them an excellent choice for a witch's familiar.

Owls
As creatures of the night, owls are commonly associated with witchcraft. The ancient Romans used the word *strix* to refer to both owls and witches, and even believed that witches could turn into owls, flying through the night to drink blood from their victims.

WHAT IS A FAMILIAR?
In European folklore, familiars were spirit guides who would offer witches help and protection. Familiars often took the shape of small animals, such as cats, ferrets, and hares. Some witches gave their familiars unusual names, such as Grizzel Greedigut, Vinegar Tom, and Pyewacket!

Black cats
Black cats are an iconic symbol of witchcraft. They became linked with the Devil in the popular imagination, leading to the superstition that black cats brought bad luck. It was thought that witches used their cat familiars for spying and causing mischief.

Fylgja
The *fylgja* are creatures of Norse mythology, said to be guardian spirits who take on the form of an animal or woman. They may come to a person in dreams or while they are awake, offering warnings of the future. The type of animal the *fylgja* appeared as could be linked to a person's character.

Chapter Five

A NEW AGE

As the modern era began, thoughts about witches continued to change. In fact, our ideas about witches are still evolving today! This era has brought revolutions, wars, and scientific and technological advances which have shaped how we see the world. Witches are an old idea, but they are also incredibly new. In this final chapter, discover how witches have evolved to be so much more than history has shown them to be, and how they might look in our magical future.

An AGE of ENLIGHTENMENT?

By the end of the 17th century, the mass witch hunts which plagued Europe were dying out. As the 18th century dawned, many people's attitudes were changing. Once, witchcraft had been seen as a real and dangerous threat. Now, it was considered fraud (deceiving or tricking), and people were punished for "pretending" to be witches. But why?

The Age of Enlightenment was a scientific and philosophical movement during the 17th and 18th centuries. It encouraged people to use reason and to search for natural explanations for things they did not understand, rather than believing in the supernatural. Enlightenment did not oppose religion, but taught that God's work could be found in rational thought and the wonder of nature. Under this new philosophy, people were less likely to believe in the power of witches and the presence of the Devil in the world, and those who did believe in those things were considered superstitious and uneducated.

The age of science

During this period, there were also advances in science and medicine, from the founding of the Royal Society for science in 1660 CE by King Charles II of England, to scientific discoveries such as Isaac Newton's theory of gravity. This scientific progress meant that some things people had believed were caused by magic, such as illness or peculiar weather, were now given scientific explanations. It is even said that in 1632, a famous physician called William Harvey cut open a "witch's familiar" to prove it was nothing more than an ordinary toad!

A change in morals and beliefs

There had always been people who objected to witch trials, but over time, more people began to feel uncomfortable with the suffering and misery trials caused. Some people wondered whether it was right to convict people with little or no evidence. Others argued that witchcraft wasn't real, and that those who confessed were mentally ill, confused, or forced into admitting their guilt through torture. People also grew suspicious of witch finders, and claimed that they were only working for their own gain.

114

The last witch hunts of Scotland

Scotland has a fierce and bloody history of witch hunts. From the North Berwick witch trials of 1590, when a group of "witches" was accused of raising a storm to drown King James VI, to the 1727 execution of Janet Horne, the last person to be executed for witchcraft in Scotland, up to 6,000 people were tried as "witches," and more than 1,500 were executed.

Changing laws

Slowly, European countries began to change their laws around witchcraft. In 1682, King Louis XIV of France released an announcement describing witchcraft as "fraudulent magic." In 1735, all previous Witchcraft Acts were withdrawn in Great Britain, and were replaced with a new act. The new Witchcraft Act stated that it was illegal to pretend to be a witch, or to carry out any type of magic, such as fortune telling. Attitudes (at least among those who made the laws) had changed, from believing that witchcraft was a real threat, to considering it a silly superstition. Witchcraft was seen as fraud.

Despite these important changes in Europe, belief in witchcraft stayed strong in many other places around the world—and still does to this day.

Between 1661 and 1662, one of the biggest witch hunts ever seen was carried out across Scotland. During this period, at least 660 people were tried under suspicion of witchcraft. The hunt began on the east coast, just outside Edinburgh, but it soon spread throughout the country, as officials were sent to root out more "witches." They used brutal methods of torture to draw confessions from people, while professional witch-prickers used sharp pins to search for the "Devil's mark" on the bodies of suspected witches.

The enormous scale of this witch hunt, and the gruesome way it played out, shocked people. They began to question the whole system.

115

MODERN BELIEFS

Although most larger witch hunts had died out by the 1700s, belief in the supernatural continued across the next 300 years, and is still present today. Sweeping changes happened around the globe, from the Industrial Revolution to the World Wars, along with ideas about witchcraft.

18TH CENTURY: FOLK MAGIC AND FRAUD

During the 1700s, scientific and philosophical movements such as the Age of Enlightenment led to doubts about witchcraft existing. Despite this, many, and perhaps even most, people in Europe still believed in witches, and the last known official trial took place in 1783 in Poland. New laws against pretending to use magic meant that cunning folk found themselves accused of fraud. Even so, people continued to visit them for their knowledge of plants and herbs.

19TH CENTURY: OCCULT OBSESSIONS

In the 19th century, scientific progress continued alongside interest in the occult. The spiritualist movement encouraged people to try to contact loved ones who had died, and secret societies practiced magical rituals. Despite laws that stated witchcraft was not real, people continued to believe in dark magic, which meant many innocent people were accused of witchcraft and treated badly.

20TH CENTURY: AGE OF ANTHROPOLOGY

During the 20th century, many anthropologists (people who study humans) studied magic in societies around the world. They had previously viewed this magic negatively, but began to see it as a sensible system that played a role in communities, solving problems and bringing people together. Views on witchcraft and women changed, and "the witch" became a powerful symbol for feminists, particularly in the UK and US. No longer seen as ugly old women, witches were shown in new ways across books, movies, and TV.

21ST CENTURY: MODERN WITCH HUNTS

Although attitudes have changed toward science and magic, many people believe in witches today. About 40 percent of people around the world say they believe in the power of witchcraft, although these numbers are very different from country to country. For many, these beliefs are linked to their religion or spiritual practices and help them connect with their ancestors. In some places, these beliefs can lead to harmful actions: when crops fail or people are suffering, witchcraft is sometimes blamed. In fact, the number of victims of modern witch hunts is now higher than the total for the early modern period.

117

SPIRITUALISM

From the mid-19th century, Europe and the US became excited about spiritualism. This movement believed it was possible to communicate with the spirits of people in the afterlife. This was done through a "medium"—someone who believed they could talk to the dead and share their messages with people who were alive. Customers would pay for meetings called séances, hoping to hear their loved ones speak again. Many found it comforting to think that spirits lived on and were watching over them. Many mediums were women, and the job offered them an opportunity for both money and fame. However, those who disapproved of spiritualism compared it to witchcraft, or suspected mediums of being liars.

OCCULTISM

This movement emerged in 19th-century Europe, and was associated with Éliphas Lévi, a magician. Occultists took a magical perspective on the world that went beyond religion or science. Lévi wrote many books about magic and ritual, and was the first to bring tarot cards into occultism. His ideas influenced several secret societies and new religions.

OCCULTISM and SPIRITUALISM

By the 18th and 19th centuries, while fewer people in the Western world believed in witchcraft, they were still fascinated by the supernatural. They combined new scientific knowledge with a longing to witness a world beyond our own. Occultist groups, attended by elite members of society, wanted to reveal the secrets of the universe. The sadness caused by the 19th century's wars and epidemics also led to the spiritualist movement, where people hoped to contact their loved ones after they had died.

SÉANCES

Meetings where people would pay a medium to try and contact the dead were called séances. We can't know for sure whether any mediums had genuine powers, but they certainly had plenty of tricks up their sleeves. Mysterious knocking on tables, moving furniture, and producing ectoplasm (ghostly goo) were all common occurrences at a séance. Mediums might also appear to go into a trance and speak with the voice of the spirit they had called upon. However, tapping noises and moving furniture could be achieved by clever systems of strings and pulleys, while ectoplasm was often nothing more than chewed-up cloth or paper!

FAKE FAIRIES AND GHASTLY GHOSTS

One of the most exciting inventions of the 19th century was photography. It didn't take long for people to try to use cameras to capture the supernatural. By layering images on top of one another, people could fake a ghostly presence. In 1917, two children were photographed playing with "fairies" in their garden. People were angry when it was revealed that the photo had been faked!

OUIJA BOARDS

Ouija boards became popular in the US in the 19th-century. Ouija boards are for "spirit writing," a practice first recorded as *Fuji* in ancient China. In 1891, the first Ouija board was released to buy. It had a ring of letters and numbers, and a pointer that a spirit could supposedly move to spell out words with the letters. Some people believed they were being contacted by their loved ones through the Ouija boards, while others saw them as harmless fun. Ouija boards now have a spookier reputation thanks to the horror film *The Exorcist*, where a Ouija board is used to connect with a demon.

MAGICAL MEN

Over the years, witchcraft has been strongly associated with women. But what about magical men? From druids to diviners, men have had many roles that deal with the strange and supernatural. Unlike witches, these men often held positions of power in their societies, and were respected for their deep wisdom and learning. This is because many cultures gave men greater opportunities. Women might also take these roles, but were often seen to be using unlearned skills, unlike educated men.

Druids

These ancient priests left no written sources behind, and are only known from Roman descriptions, so people have been free to imagine, reinterpret, and reinvent them ever since. Druids seemed to be knowledgeable and important members of society. They were interested in the power of the natural world, and helped connect their communities with the gods, as well as acting as teachers and judges. It is thought that the oak tree and mistletoe plant were particularly sacred to them.

Wizards

Also known as magicians, warlocks, or sorcerers, wizards are people with magical powers. They appear in myths and folklore from all around the world, but are sometimes real people too. One such person was John Dee, an English mathematician and astrologer, who gave magical advice to Queen Elizabeth I. Wizards are also common in fantasy books, movies, and role-playing games. They can have the ability to cast spells, brew potions, or predict the future. Often, they appear as wise old men who advise or oppose the hero of a story.

Soothsayers and astrologers

People with the ability to predict the future are known as soothsayers. In ancient Rome, they were a type of priest. One story tells of a soothsayer who warned Julius Caesar to "beware the Ides (fifteenth) of March." Caesar didn't listen, and was murdered on that day. Astrologers are a type of soothsayer who use the movements of the stars and planets to predict the future.

Diviners

Dowsers, or diviners, are people with the magical ability to find hidden things—especially water or other things underground. To find something, they often use a tool called a dowsing rod or twig, and walk slowly across an area. When they are above their target, the dowsing rod dips or twitches in their hands. This practice dates back to the ancient Babylonians and Egyptians, who used split reeds for dowsing. The Catholic Church was suspicious of the practice, so they banned it.

Necromancers

These magical people can summon the spirits of those who have died, and were active all across the ancient world, from Rome to China. In the medieval period, the Christian Church was suspicious of necromancy—it believed the spirits summoned were demons, so they condemned it as harmful magic. During this time, the practice involved complicated rituals including magic circles, conjurations, and sacrifices.

121

BRUJERÍA

Brujería is the Spanish word for witchcraft. In Latin America, it describes a mixture of religious and magical practices that have been influenced by Indigenous traditions, African rituals, and Catholic beliefs. *Brujería* can involve herbalism, prayer, spells, curses, cleansing rituals, charms, and divination.

THE HISTORY OF BRUJERÍA

Indigenous peoples living in the Americas had strong spiritual traditions, alongside extensive knowledge about native plants and medicine. In the 16th century, Spanish invaders brought different cultures into contact with each other. The rituals and beliefs of the Catholic Spanish invaders, enslaved West Africans from the Caribbean, and Indigenous populations in the Americas blended to form *brujería*. The Spanish Catholics in power wanted everyone to become Christian. They were afraid of different beliefs, so people who practiced *brujería* were accused of witchcraft by the Mexican Inquisition. Despite this, *brujería* survived and is still practiced today.

BRUJERÍA INCLUDES MANY DIFFERENT BELIEFS, RITUALS, AND TRADITIONS.

SANTERÍA

Santería is an Afro-Caribbean religion, whose name means "the way of the Saints." Some followers prefer the name *Regla de Ocha*. It is influenced by West African Yoruba culture and Catholicism. Between the 16th and 19th centuries, enslaved African people were taken to the Americas in the Atlantic slave trade and were forced to be Catholics. Many resisted by disguising worship of their own gods as worship of Catholic saints, which became Santería. It was viewed as witchcraft by people in power, so they tried to stamp it out, but Santería still flourishes today.

Brujería has become popular again, especially among young Latinx people. Many see it as a way to connect to their history and appreciate the universe. People who have been treated unfairly can use *brujería* to stand up for themselves. Some people who practice *brujería* like the title of brujx, but others choose not to use it due to its negative history. It's important to remember that *brujería* means something different to everyone who embraces it.

The orisha Oshun

ORISHAS

Orishas are the deities (gods or spirits) of Santería, which also has a main creator god, known as Olodumare. There are hundreds of different *orishas*, and followers of Santería believe that everyone has a special connection with one. Some popular *orishas* include Yemaya, the mother of oceans and lakes; Oya, queen of storms and rain; and Oshun, the *orisha* of fresh water, femininity, and love. Oshun is adored by her followers, who leave offerings of yellow fruits, sunflowers, and honey in her honor.

WICCA

Also known as "The Craft," Wicca is a modern pagan religion with strong links to nature. Many followers identify as witches, follow seasonal celebrations, or worship a Horned God and Triple Goddess, who represent different aspects of nature, or various other deities. It comes in hundreds of forms, some as individual as a single person. Despite its reputation throughout history, Wiccan witchcraft is positive.

SYMBOLOGY, BELIEFS, AND RITUALS

Wiccans are the followers of Wicca. They believe in the power of nature, which is represented in many of their symbols, rituals, and traditions. The Pentacle, a five-pointed star, represents the five elements: Earth, Air, Fire, Water, and Spirit. Their rituals also celebrate nature, often taking place outside. These rituals may involve music, dance, prayer, or meditation. Wiccans do not believe in cursing or harmful magic. They live by the motto "If it harm none, do what you will," which means that they are free to do whatever they want, as long as it doesn't hurt anyone or anything. There are no other rules in Wicca.

IF IT HARM NONE, DO WHAT YOU WILL.

Wicca was once thought to be an ancient religion, but it is actually very modern. It was developed in Britain from about the 1920s, when people were interested in the ancient rites and practices of their ancestors. The founder, Gerald Brousseau Gardner, introduced Wicca to the public in the 1950s, alongside a magical text he had written: the *Book of Shadows*. Over the next few decades, Wicca spread. During the 1970s, it gained links to feminism and the environment. Today, there are many different branches of Wicca, each with their own set of beliefs and rituals.

WICCA HAS STRONG LINKS TO FEMINISM AND THE ENVIRONMENT.

LIFE AFTER DEATH

Wiccans believe in reincarnation—the idea that our soul is born again in a different body. This is also a central belief of many other religions, such as Hinduism, Buddhism, Sikhism, and Jainism. Wiccans believe that, after death, the soul travels to a place called Summerland. Some see Summerland as a land of eternal summer, where there is no pain or suffering. Once there, the soul rests until it is ready to be born again into its next life.

CELEBRATIONS

The Wiccan calendar is known as the "Wheel of the Year." The celebrations mark important moments in Earth's journey around the sun. Known as Sabbats, celebrations may involve feasting, cleaning, giving thanks, or remembering ancestors.

Yule
A celebration of the Winter Solstice—the shortest day of the year.

Imbolc
Imbolc celebrates the coming of spring.

Ostara
A celebration of the Spring Equinox and new beginnings.

Beltane
Beltane welcomes the start of summer.

Litha
In honor of the Summer Solstice—the longest day of the year.

Lammas
Also known as Lughnasadh, the beginning of the harvest season.

Mabon
Mabon celebrates the Autumn Equinox, as the season turns into winter.

Samhain
A Celtic festival that marks the passing of the year.

TAROT

Cartomancy is divination that uses a special pack of cards. The most common form is tarot, where each card has a different symbol and meaning. A tarot reader shuffles the cards, invites a person to select some, then lays them out in a spread. The cards chosen help the person answer a question, and a card's meaning depends on whether it is the right way up or upside down ("in reverse").

The Fool
A carefree young man, The Fool is a symbol of innocence and represents new beginnings. When reversed, it can suggest recklessness and risk-taking.

The Sun
The Sun is a joyful card that represents success, contentment, and positivity. In reverse, it may suggest unrealistic expectations or negativity.

The Magician
The Magician is a magical card that represents creativity and the link between the natural and supernatural realms. In reverse, it can hint at trickery.

Death
Although it may seem scary, the Death card can be very positive. It represents change, transformation, and moving forward. In reverse, it suggests resistance to change.

THE ORIGINS OF TAROT
The first references to tarot came from Italy in the 15th century, when it was a card game played for entertainment. In the 18th century, occultism (study of the supernatural) became popular in France. French occultists claimed that tarot cards had magical links to ancient Egypt. Soon, special tarot decks were produced for occult purposes, and they've been used for fortune telling ever since.

126

The Tower
A card of change, The Tower suggests a sudden and dramatic event, either good or bad. In reverse, it can mean you want to avoid change or disaster.

THE TOWER

Justice
A symbol of fairness, Justice represents truth and honesty. In reverse, it may mean the opposite—dishonesty, unfairness, and injustice.

JUSTICE

The High Priestess
The High Priestess is a mysterious card that represents sacred knowledge and listening to your inner voice. In reverse, it may mean feeling unbalanced and not understanding your feelings.

THE HIGH PRIESTESS

SPREAD LAYOUTS
Tarot readers use different patterns called spreads to answer different questions.

The Three Card Spread is the simplest tarot spread, often representing the past, present, and future.

The Horseshoe Spread uses seven cards. It looks at obstacles and influences as well as the answers to questions.

The Pentagram Spread has five points, which represent the elements.

Three Card Spread

Seven Card Horseshoe

The Pentagram

Jade
Purity and immortality

Since ancient times, jade has been important in Chinese culture. During the early dynasties, it was used only by noble people, who were often buried with the gemstone. It was known as the "essence of heaven and Earth," and was linked to purity, virtue, and immortality. Jade objects still play an important role in Chinese culture today.

The MAGIC of CRYSTALS

While crystals do not have a direct link to witchcraft, cultures around the world have long believed in their magical powers. The ancient Sumerians, who used stones such as lapis lazuli in their medicine, were the first to write about the power of crystals. In the 1980s, crystals became popular once more, and many people still believe in their abilities to heal and protect today.

Obsidian
Divination

Obsidian is a dark volcanic glass that is created when lava cools and solidifies before crystals have time to form in it. The glass has the sharpest cutting edge found in nature, and was important to many cultures of Mesoamerica, especially the Aztecs. The creator god, Tezcatlipoca, was believed to use an obsidian mirror to divine the future. The English wizard John Dee had an obsidian scrying glass—a mirror used for seeing prophecies or visions.

Hematite
Invincibility

Hematite is a common gemstone found in rocks and soil. In ancient Babylon, it was carried by warriors who believed it would give them superhuman strength. Ancient Greeks painted their bodies with crushed hematite before going into battle.

Chrysolite
Protection

Chrysolite, also known as peridot, is a green-gold gem, known by the ancient Egyptians as the "stone of the sun." Peridot was so valuable to the Egyptians that they kept the island where it was found a secret! It was believed that peridot amulets provided protection from night terrors.

Rose quartz
Love

This pink gemstone is a type of quartz, found across most continents. Known as the "love stone," it is connected with romance. In ancient Hindu scriptures, rose quartz was thought to help open and balance the heart chakra—an energy center within the body.

The WITCH in MODERN MEDIA

People have always been fascinated by witches, so it's no surprise that they appear in some of our earliest forms of media—from ancient epics and fairy tales to paintings and plays. Whether as a kind enchantress, evil crone, or intelligent student, the way different societies portray witches can tell us a lot about how they view magic and women.

BOOKS AND PLAYS

In 15th- to 18th-century Europe, witches in books were usually powerful dark magicians, such as the three witches in Shakespeare's *Macbeth* who brew potions and meddle with the future. In the 19th century, witches in the stories of Hans Christian Andersen and the Brothers Grimm were exaggerated, attacking the innocent and eventually getting punished. By the 20th century, witches were more varied, such as the Good Witch of the North, who helps Dorothy in L. Frank Baum's *The Wonderful Wizard of Oz*. Other stories showed witches as brave children, who became role models for young readers.

ART

In 15th- to 18th-century Europe, artists such as Albrecht Dürer and Lucas Cranach portrayed witches as frightening, ugly old women who rode goats, brewed potions, and attended Sabbaths. They encouraged fears about witches.

Modern art often shows them in a very different light. *The Magic Circle*, painted by John William Waterhouse in 1886, shows a witch as feminine and proud. Artists such as Virginia Lupu and Francis F. Denny have photographed women who call themselves witches. Unlike most witches throughout history, the women are shown in the way they would like to be, and their images are very powerful.

The Magic Circle by John William Waterhouse

FILM, TV, AND THEATER

The invention of film and TV has seen witches take to the big screen. Some of the earliest movies were Disney versions of fairy tales, such as *Snow White*, *Sleeping Beauty*, and *The Little Mermaid*, where witches were portrayed as evil and jealous women. Over time, they evolved into the good-hearted or silly characters of films such as *Kiki's Delivery Service* and *Hocus Pocus*. Modern adaptations of old stories, such as *Maleficent* and *Wicked*, went even further, giving "evil" witches a sympathetic backstory to add a feminist twist to tales.

Kiki's Delivery Service

WITCHES FIGHT BACK

Throughout history, people have been mistreated for their use of magic, whether real or imagined. Many of these people were innocent victims, whose only crime was not fitting in. Now, for some, magic and witchcraft have become a way of fighting back. From feminists to climate campaigners, "the witch" has transformed into a powerful symbol for change.

WITCHCRAFT AND FEMINISM

The history of witchcraft and magic have strong links to modern feminist movements. Some feminists in the 1970s saw the witch trials that swept through Europe in the 15th to 18th centuries as cruel attacks on knowledgeable women, such as traditional healers or midwives. Although the truth is more complicated than this, some feminists have continued to identify with witches, who they see as symbols of feminine strength. From Sabrina to Circe, "the witch" has become a modern feminist icon—a powerful figure who is not afraid to stand out.

POLITICAL RESISTANCE

Witchcraft has managed to find its way into modern politics. Practicing witches have used their voices to call for change, from taking part in protests to weaving spells to stop political figures from doing harmful things. Sometimes groups of witches gather together to cast spells to help people in need, such as those affected by war or natural disasters. Most modern witchcraft isn't about casting curses, but is used to inspire kindness and positivity.

CLIMATE ACTIVISM

As the threat of climate change has grown, modern witchcraft has become linked with eco-activism (standing up for the protection of nature). People who practice green witchcraft believe that caring for the Earth is very important. They may be involved with different aspects of eco-activism, from encouraging people to recycle to attending protests against fossil fuels.

RECLAIMING HISTORY

During the colonial period, Europeans had many wrong beliefs about the traditions of Indigenous people, and punished some of them as "witches." For the relatives of these victims living today, recovering their magical and spiritual traditions can be very powerful. One example of this is people who practice *brujería*, a Latin American blend of Indigenous knowledge, Catholic beliefs, and West African spiritualism.

INCLUSIVE WITCHCRAFT

For many people, modern witchcraft can offer a safe place to discover who they are and what they want from their lives. Some people identify as witches as a way to embrace their personal powers in a world that treats them unfairly. Practices linked to modern witchcraft, such as meditation, self-care, and work in local communities, can also have positive impacts on people and their communities.

GREEN WITCHCRAFT

Green witchcraft or "eco-witchcraft" is a modern form of witchcraft. It has reimagined some of the past techniques of healers and cunning folk to create something new. It combines magic with a deep respect for the natural world, and can be used for personal well-being, to promote climate activism, and to create peace between humans and nature. Green witchcraft shares similarities with Wicca, but green witches follow their own traditions and beliefs.

THE ELEMENTS

Each of the four natural elements—earth, air, wind, and fire—is believed to have its own special qualities. Some green witches draw on the elements' different energies to connect with the natural world for rituals or spells. This can involve collecting objects such as shells, leaves, and gemstones, or setting up shrines dedicated to the elements.

NATURAL ALLIES

Green witches believe in working with the power of nature—from living in tune with the seasons and celebrating the natural turns of the year, to observing local wildlife and growing their knowledge of plants and trees. The sun and moon are also important: the sun represents life and growth, while the moon is a symbol of change and mystery. An eco-witch might carry out different rituals during each of the eight phases of the moon.

SUSTAINABILITY

Green witchcraft focuses on respecting and caring for the natural world, so sustainable and eco-friendly practices are very important. Eco-witches believe that if they provide healing and love to Earth, it will do the same for them. They might focus their rituals or energy on climate activism, such as supporting protests against deforestation or fossil fuels, or joining environmental action groups.

CONNECTING WITH EARTH

Some green witches make use of spirituality, mindfulness, and meditation practices to strengthen their connection to Earth and improve their mental health. "Grounding" is one way of doing this. It involves making deliberate physical contact with Earth, such as standing on the grass in your bare feet or feeling the bark of a tree with your hand, and trying to absorb its energy into your body to bring a sense of peace and well-being. Other rituals include journaling, gardening, and walking in nature.

COMMUNITY

Green witches believe in building harmony between themselves, other humans, and the planet. Giving back to Earth and the community they live in is one way to restore balance. This might involve volunteering with local groups or creating safe spaces for local plants and animals. This slow and purposeful living is the backbone of eco-witchcraft.

The FUTURE of WITCHES

Witchcraft is still viewed with fear or superstition in some cultures, but in others it is linked to self-expression and has become a form of spirituality. For some, it provides a connection with nature and the Earth, or it can be used as a way of respecting and remembering their history. But what might magic and witchcraft look like in the future?

SHIFTING THINKING

In many modern cultures, witches have been making their way into people's hearts through fantastical stories. Attitudes toward women and religion have slowly improved as people have received better education and become more interested in embracing different ways of thinking. However, there are also places where magic or magical women are still viewed as a threat.

UNCOVERING HISTORY

Thanks to historians and archaeologists, we are constantly learning more about the history of witchcraft. Their research has uncovered ancient artifacts and documents that help us understand the traditions and beliefs of other cultures. Discovering more about the history of witchcraft lets us dream about its future and bring some of its best traditions back to life.

MAGIC AND SCIENCE

Developments in science mean we can now explain things that were blamed on witchcraft in the past. However, some modern magic has adapted to exist alongside these incredible advances. Some people practice eco-witchcraft to try to help the fight against climate change. Meanwhile, plants from ancient healing spells are sometimes used in modern medicine, and scientists are constantly working to find cures for illnesses in nature.

MAGIC EVERYWHERE

If you look around, you can find magic everywhere. Embracing it can help you to make the most of your daily life—from basking in the beauty of nature to cherishing the company of your friends. If we all take time to respect other people's beliefs and traditions, and remember the past, it will help us appreciate the present and shape a future that is better for everyone.

WHAT DOES "WITCH" MEAN to YOU?

The history of witchcraft has taken us on a journey around the world, from ancient times to the present day. Along the way, "the witch" has transformed from a dreaded goddess and feared foe, to a valued neighbor and feminist icon. Have your ideas about witchcraft changed too?

WHERE DO WITCHES COME FROM?

As you have seen, witches are not just from one place or time in history—they have played an important role in most cultures and can be found all around the globe. The earliest references to witches come from as far back as Mesopotamia, more than 5,000 years ago! From ancient China to Greek mythology, Mayan civilization to modern Korea, witches appear all over the world in many different forms, and they never fail to fascinate.

ARE WITCHES REAL?

There are many points in history where most people believed that witches were real. From prehistory to the present, the threat of dark magic was something that many societies took seriously. Now, although fewer people believe in sorcery, and witches are more likely to be found in books or movies than courtrooms, many people and cultures consider witches to be real. Some fear them as workers of evil, while others embrace doing magic themselves.

Whether you believe in witches or not probably depends on if you believe in magic. Whatever you think, it is wise to always keep an open mind and try to understand other people's beliefs.

ARE WITCHES POWERFUL?

In myths and legends from around the world, witches possess powers to transform their shape, brew deadly potions, control the weather, and more. People have even believed that witches could summon demons to act as their servants. This meant that people also thought witches were weak, because they gave in to temptation and agreed to serve the Devil. People found ways to repel witches, such as protective charms, spells, or amulets, and healers would cure illnesses caused by witches' dark magic.

ARE WITCHES ALWAYS WOMEN?

In the past, beliefs about female characteristics meant that people accused of witchcraft were usually women, and "witch" is often used to mean a woman who practices magic. Many people have now reclaimed the word "witch," using it to represent female power, strength, and standing up for rights. But, across history and in the present day, witches can be male, female, or neither!

WHAT IS MAGIC?

Magic is usually defined as supernatural power, but, as we have seen, it can be many things. It can be prayer and rituals, or appreciating nature. It can involve spells and incantations, or simple meditation and healing. Magic can bring communities together and connect them with ancestors, or it can be a source of strength for people who do not fit in. How someone experiences magic is up to them!

SO ... WHAT IS A WITCH?

There is no one way to define a "witch." From Joan of Arc to Circe, Empress Chen Jiao to Baba Yaga, witchcraft is as complicated and diverse as we are! Witches can be strong or weak, old or young, good or bad. They can be someone proud of their craft or someone falsely accused. They can be real or fictional, from anywhere and any time. Witches can be anything!

What does "witch" mean to you?

139

GLOSSARY

AMULET
Magical pendant worn to protect from harm

ASTROLOGY
Way to predict events based on the positions of the stars, planets, sun, and moon

AZTEC
Civilization which existed in the 15th and early 16th centuries in what is now central and southern Mexico

BALINESE
Group of people native to the Indonesian island of Bali

BETROTHAL
Engagement to be married

BLACK DEATH
Plague that happened in Europe between 1347 and 1351

CELTS
Group of ancient people that lived across Europe from the 2nd millennium BCE

CHARIOT
Two-wheeled vehicle pulled by horses

CLIMATE CHANGE
Change in temperature and weather across the Earth that can be natural or caused by human activity

CONDEMNED
Sentenced to a punishment

CONQUISTADOR
Spanish or Portuguese soldier who conquered new territory

CUNNING FOLK
People who practiced traditional folk magic such as healing or helpful charms

DEITY
Sacred supernatural being such as a god or goddess

DISEMBODIED
Separated from the body

DIVINATION
Art of seeing the future

DIVINER
Person who has special powers to see into the future or find the location of water, minerals, or other things underground

DOMESTIC
Relating to the household

DYNASTY
Series of rulers who are all from the same family

ENCHANTRESS
Woman who can perform magic

ENSLAVED
Forced to work without pay

EQUINOX
One of two moments in the year when the sun is exactly above the Equator and day and night are the same length

EXILE
Banish from one's home or country

EXORCISE
Process of getting rid of an evil spirit

FEMINIST
Person who believes that men and women are equal

FOLK HEALER
Person who treats sick people with traditional medicine and magic

FOLKLORE
Traditional beliefs, stories, and customs shared by a particular culture or group of people

FUNERAL PYRE
Pile of wood used for burning a dead body

HALLUCINATION
Seeing or hearing something that isn't there

HEIR
Person, such as a child or grandchild, who is entitled to inherit things from another person when that person dies

HERBALISM
Study of the use of plants in medicine

HERESY
Disagreeing with a popular belief or religion

INCANTATION
Words that are used as a magical spell

INDIGENOUS
The people that originally lived in a region or country

INQUISITOR
Person who investigates people or things that go against Catholicism

LATINX
Latin American person of any gender

LEGEND
Story from the past that is sometimes historical and sometimes not true

MAGISTRATE
Person who acts as a judge in court

MAYAN
Civilization that existed from ancient times in what is now Central America and Mexico

MESOAMERICA
Historic and cultural region extending from central Mexico to Costa Rica

MIDWIFERY
Job that assists women in childbirth

MINISTER
Religious leader, usually in the Christian Church

MYTH
Traditional story which often explains the origins of a group of people or an event, and is sometimes not true

NECROMANCER
Person who claims to communicate with the dead

NOBLE
Of high birth or rank

NYMPH
Magical woman or girl who is connected to nature such as water, trees, or mountains

OCCULTISM
Belief in certain supernatural powers

OINTMENT
Substance that is rubbed on the skin, usually for medical purposes

PAGAN
Person who follows Paganism, a religion with multiple gods inspired by ancient beliefs and rituals

PAPYRUS
Grasslike plant that is pressed to create paper

PEDDLER
Person who travels and sells things

POPE
Head of the Catholic Church

PRACTITIONER
Person who is skilled in a job or activity

RUNE
Character in an alphabet used by European people from about the 3rd to the 13th centuries

SÁMI
Indigenous group of people who live in northern parts of Finland, Norway, Sweden, and Russia

SEER
Person who is said to be able to see into the future

SHAMAN
Person who has supernatural powers and can connect with spirits

SHAPE-SHIFT
Transform into a different form or shape

SHINTO
Traditional Japanese religion which believes in more than one god and is connected to nature

SLAVIC
Set of languages from regions of central, southeastern, and eastern Europe, including Poland, Croatia, Ukraine, and Russia

SOLSTICE
One of two moments in the year when the sun reaches its farthest point from the Equator, and either day or night is at its longest

SPIRITUAL
Relating to deep feelings or beliefs, religion, the supernatural, or the human spirit or soul

SUPERNATURAL
Caused by something that cannot be explained by science or nature

TALISMAN
Object with religious or magical powers which can heal or protect from harm

UNDERWORLD
Place where people are thought to go after they die in some religions and belief systems

VIRTUE
Quality of being good

WIDOW
Woman whose spouse has died

YIN-YANG
Concept from Chinese philosophy where two forces with opposite personalities work together to make up all aspects of life

ZODIAC WHEEL
Circular diagram that represents the 12 zodiac signs—formations of stars that some people think we can use to make predictions about humans

INDEX

A
African culture 23, 78-79, 108-109, 122
Age of Enlightenment 114-115, 116
alchemists 77
amulets 27, 62
animals 13, 35, 71, 111
anthropology 117
Aphrodite's herb 48
astrology 29, 53, 69, 121
Atharvaveda 22
augury 69
Azande people 108
Aztec Empire 128

B
Baba Yaga 19, 54
Bell Witch, The 18
binding spells 44
Book of the Dead 22, 27
books 22-23, 83, 130
Brigid 72
broomsticks 13, 67, 70

C
Caldwell, Christian 90
Canada 58, 106, 107
cap of invisibility 98
Caribbean 78-79, 97, 123
carpets, flying 71
cartomancy 126
Catholicism 78, 94, 122-123
cats 13, 35, 111
cauldrons 66
Celtic mythology 69, 72-73
censers 99
Ceridwen 18, 72
chalices 67
charms 62-63
Chen Jiao, Empress 32-33
Chen Jinggu 18, 31
China 30-33, 99, 128
Christianity 17, 52, 92, 104
chrysanthemums 65
chrysolite 129
Cintamani stone 99
Circe 18, 36, 38-39
climate change 104, 133, 134
colonialism 96-97
crystals 128-129
cunning folk 76-77
curanderas 94
curses 41, 44-45, 100

D
datura (thorn apple) 43, 49
deadly nightshade 42
death 27
demons 17, 61
Dickson, John 90
divination 34, 68-69, 122, 126
diviners 121
druids 120
ducking 88
Dzunukwa 58

E
eco-witchcraft 134-135
Egypt, ancient 22, 26-27, 62, 129
elements 59, 134
Europe 54-57, 72-74, 77, 84-85

F
fairies 119
familiars 111
feminism 132
film 13, 131
flight 70-71, 93
Frau Perchta 54
Freyja 57
fylgja 111

G
ghosts 119
ginseng 43
gods 17, 26, 56, 57
Greece, ancient 22, 36-39, 46-47, 61
  potions and medicines 48, 129
green witchcraft 134-135
Grimhildr 19
grimoires 67

H
hammers 98
Harut and Marut 29
healers 76-77, 96-97
Hecate 37
heka 26
hematite 129
henbane 43
herbs 42-43, 48
Hercules 49
Hinduism 22
history of witchcraft 14-15
hoodoo 42, 76
Hopkins, Matthew 90

I
I Ching 69
incantation bowls 63
India 22, 49, 129
Indigenous peoples 96-97, 110, 122-123, 133
  of North America 58, 61, 91, 106-107
inquisitions 94
invisibility 98
Ireland 72, 73, 74
Islam, ancient 28-29, 77

J, K
jade 128
James I, King 100
Japan 34-35, 45, 48, 98
Jenny Greenteeth 19
Jinn 28
Joan of Arc 86-87
Judaism 19, 22, 53, 92
Juju 109
kitsune 34
Korean culture 77
Kyteler, Alice 74-75

L
La Befana 19, 55
Lamia 61
Latin America 122-123
La Xtabay 58
Leyaks 110
Lilith 19
literature 22-23, 83, 130
lotus root 48
Louhi 19, 110
love-in-idleness 48

love spells 48-49
Lutzelfrau 55

M

magical objects 98-99
Magical Papyri 22
Maka people 108
Manananggal 60
mandrake 49
marks 62, 88
Mayan mythology 23, 58
Medea 19, 46-47, 64, 128
media 12, 130-131
medicine 27, 42-43
Medieval Period 52-53
Melusine 19
men 120-121
Mesopotamia 24-25, 29, 62
Mexico 94-95
mice 111
Michaelis, Sebastien 91
Minthe's mixture 48
mirrors 66
Morrigan, The 18, 73
mortar and pestles 71
mothers 59
Mother Shipton 77
Mudang 77
mugwort 43
mushrooms 65

N

naguals 110
nature 64-65, 124-125, 134-135
necromancers 121
Nicneven 18
Norns 56
Noroi 45

Norse mythology 19, 56-57, 111
North America 78-79, 102-103
    Indigenous peoples 58, 61, 91, 106-107

O

obsidian 128
occultism 116, 118-119
Odysseus 38
ointments 70
oneiromancy 68
oracles 36
orishas 123
Ouija boards 119
owls 111
Oya 18

P

Pachamama 18
palmistry 68
Pendle Witch Trials 100-101
Picatrix 23
plants 42-43, 64-65
Pollock, Maggie 107
Popol Vuh 23
potions 42, 48-49
pricking 89
protection 25, 62-63, 64, 128
pumpkins 64

R

Rémy, Nicholas 91
Rhiannon 73
Rome, ancient 40-41, 60
rose quartz 129
rune casting 69

S

Sabbath 92-93
Sacred Corpus of Ifá 23
saints 17, 123
Salem Witch Trials 102-103
Sangomas 109
Santeria 123
science 77, 114, 137
Scotland 115
séances 119
seven-league boots 99
shamans 76
shape-shifters 110
shoes 63
Snow Queen 59
Snow White 59
soothsayers 121
Spain 23, 94
spells 44, 48-49, 67
    see also curses
spiritualism 118-119
stepmothers 59
stereotypes 12-13
Strix 60
superstitions 63, 69
symbology 62, 124, 126

T

Tanakh, the 22
tarot 126-127
tasseomancy 68
Tenskwatawa 91
thorn apple (datura) 43, 49
timeline of witchcraft 14-1
Tlahuelpuchi 61
toads 111
touch tests 89
transportation 70-71
trees 64-65

V, W

vampires 61
vervain 42
Vodou 78-79
Völva 56
von Ehrenberg, Philipp Adolf 90
Wales 72, 73
wands 67
Wicca 93, 124-125
witch cake 89
witch hunting 82-83, 90-91, 94, 115
    causes 104-105
    methods 88-89
    trials 74, 84-85, 87, 100-103
Witch of Endor 19
wizards 120
women 10-11, 83, 87, 105
woodland 58
wormwood 43

Y, Z

Yamauba 18
yōkai 34
Yoruba people 23
Zhalmauyz Kempir 19

ACKNOWLEDGMENTS

DK would like to thank:
Laura Galán-Wells and Sarosh Arif
for sensitivity reading, Peter Gee for
proofreading, Elizabeth Wise for indexing,
and Sakshi Saluja and Manpreet Kaur
for picture research assistance.

The publisher would like to thank the following for their
kind permission to reproduce their photographs:

(Key: a-above; b-below/bottom; c-center;
f-far; l-left; r-right; t-top)

22 University of Toronto Libraries: Atharva-Veda samhita: translated with a critical and exegetical commentary by William Dwight Whitney. Revised and brought nearer to completion and edited by Charles Rockwell Lanman (bl). **25 Bridgeman Images:** Photo © Photo Josse (br). © **The Trustees of the British Museum. All rights reserved:** (cl). **The Metropolitan Museum of Art:** Bequest of W. Gedney Beatty, 1941 (tr). **27 Alamy Stock Photo:** Art Directors & TRIP / Helene Rogers (tc); Portis Imaging (cl). **The Art Institute of Chicago:** Gift of Henry H. Getty and Charles L. Hutchinson (ftr). **The Metropolitan Museum of Art:** Rogers Fund, 1936 (tr). **41 Mike Peel:** (t). **42 Dreamstime.com:** Manfred Ruckszio (cla). **42-43 Dreamstime.com:** Nadezhda Andriyakhina (c). **43 Dreamstime.com:** Jianghongyan (bc); Spectral-design (tc); Kazakovmaksim (tr); Pavel Parmenov (crb). **49 Dreamstime.com:** Picture Partners (ca); Zurijeta (tl); Manfred Ruckszio (cla). **63 Alamy Stock Photo:** Zev Radovan (br). **83 Alamy Stock Photo:** Jimlop collection (tr). **Dreamstime.com:** Yuriy Chaban (cl). **128 Alamy Stock Photo:** The Museum of East Asian Art / Heritage Images (cl). **Dreamstime.com:** Richpav (bl). **129 Dreamstime.com:** Dafnanb (br); Asmus Koefoed (tr); Fokinol (ca); Ekaterina Kriminskaia (clb). **131 Alamy Stock Photo:** steeve-x-art (cra). **GKIDS:** © 1989 Eiko Kadono / Hayao Miyazaki / Studio Ghibli, N (bl)

ABOUT THE AUTHOR

Hazel Atkinson is an author from the North East of England. From childhood experiments with "potion-making" to studying the history of witchcraft in college, she has always been fascinated by stories of magic and mystery.

She currently lives in the wild northern county of Northumberland with her husband, son, and their very spoiled cat. *The Extraordinary History of Witches* is her first children's book.

ABOUT THE ILLUSTRATOR

Camelia is a Vietnamese illustrator and an art director.

She graduated in graphic design and is now a freelance illustrator based in Hanoi. Her work focuses mostly on telling stories through human bodies, bold colors, and decorative frames. She has won a lot of international awards for her works and has dabbled in the animation field as an art director.

She is now working as a freelance illustrator and enjoying her life creating art at home, all while snuggling with her dog and constantly trying to find good working cafes in the city.

ABOUT THE CONSULTANT

Diane Purkiss is Professor of English literature at the University of Oxford, and fellow of Keble College. She is an expert on the history of witchcraft. Her most recent book on the subject is *The Museum of Witchcraft*.